Making Sense of the Hebrew Bible

Making Sense of the Hebrew Bible

Robert A. Butterfield
Foreword by Vitor Westhelle

WIPF & STOCK · Eugene, Oregon

MAKING SENSE OF THE HEBREW BIBLE

Copyright © 2016 Robert A. Butterfield. All rights reserved. Except for brief quotations in critical publications or reviews, no part of this book may be reproduced in any manner without prior written permission from the publisher. Write: Permissions, Wipf and Stock Publishers, 199 W. 8th Ave., Suite 3, Eugene, OR 97401.

Wipf & Stock
An Imprint of Wipf and Stock Publishers
199 W. 8th Ave., Suite 3
Eugene, OR 97401

www.wipfandstock.com

PAPERBACK ISBN: 978-1-5362-0040-1
HARDCOVER ISBN: 978-1-5362-0042-5
EBOOK ISBN: 978-1-5362-0041-8

Manufactured in the U.S.A.   DECEMBER 5, 2016

To University of Chicago professor Bernard Weinberg, in loving memory.

Contents

Foreword by Vítor Westhelle | ix
Acknowledgments | xiii

Introduction | 1
1 In the Beginning | 3
2 Stringing Stories Together with Metaphors | 12
3 Israel's Real History | 25
4 More about Structure | 44
5 Messianic Expectation | 52
6 Socio-religious Origins of Jesus of Nazareth | 55
7 Jewish Ethics and the Ethics of Jesus of Nazareth | 58
8 Role of Festivals in Postexilic Israel | 67
9 Some Practical Implications | 74
10 Destruction/Re-creation in the New Testament | 77

Glossary | 99
Bibliography | 105

Foreword

BOOKS CAN FURTHER SCHOLARLY research and implement our archival memory; they may also provide us with monumentally new interpretative theories, or else rehash old teaching to provide new didactical tools for presenting them. Outside of that, there is plenty of hogwash that does nothing but clutter bookshelves. Robert Butterfield's *Making Sense of the Hebrew Bible* is none of the above. It does not pretend to bring to light new data offering a new hermeneutical theory for how to read the Hebrew Bible; neither is it a rehashing of established teachings in new language. Above all, it most definitely is not a work to be disparaged. This little book, whose size is in inverse proportion to its significance, presents us with something else: a text that reads the Hebrew Bible by choosing selected but crucial pericopes as a cohesive narrative of disconcerting bluntness about the human condition and the perils and promise of faith in a God who creates because this God wants partners.

Making Sense of the Hebrew Bible is distinct in its presentation of the Hebrew Scriptures as the story of a conversation of God with God's people and of their response, which is often a failure in communication, with tragic and destructive consequences. From this communication emerges the template of the biblical narrative. The editorial choice of placing the second creation story by the Word (Gen 1:1—2:4a) at the very beginning sets the pattern in motion.

FOREWORD

God communes with the whole of the created world, but what follows is the destruction of this communion, and out of God's steadfast love (*hesed*) there is a re-creation. The whole Hebrew Bible is framed within this paradigm of creation/destruction/re-creation, or, if you will, conception, humiliation, and exaltation.

To present the Bible as the story of God communicating with God's creatures in love and of the recurring failure of the human creature to respond to this steadfast love is to invite the reader of the Bible to enter into this very conversation and respond to God appropriately. The goal of the interpretation presented here is therefore not an exercise in a new biblical hermeneutics, but rather a restoration of the function of the Bible as interpreting the human condition by placing us creatures in relationship with God. In other words, the Bible is itself the interpreter. With this move, Butterfield heeds to the biblical principle of the Reformers. Yet he does so in a radical ecumenical spirit, while steering clear of all the baggage of dogmatic layers that the history of doctrinal, authoritative teachings by synagogue and church alike has laid upon the Bible. This use of the Bible unencumbered by doctrine avoids harmonizing domestication of the text, welcomes its disturbing dissonances, and affirms diversity.

Throughout the book this ecumenical spirit surfaces in two maneuvers. While the first is tactical in nature, the second is strategic. The tactical maneuver is to insert Christianity into the history of Israel as one of its decisive moments—but not the only one. By dedicating the last chapter to the book of Mark in the New Testament, Butterfield is able to demonstrate that Jesus is the representative of true Judaism, which deviated from what then had become "normative Judaism"—centered on the temple, as earlier it had focused on kingship—but nevertheless faithful to the biblical tradition. That Jesus is the representative of true Judaism does not imply supersession, for the history of messianic manifestation remains open. Implicitly rebuked is the once-for-all (*ephapax*) claim of Christianity as a religious option that brings to an end the history of Israel. By the same token "normative Judaism" is chastised when it does not acknowledge Jesus as a bearer of the messianic promise, much as the patriarchs, Moses, Elijah, and other prophets were. Jesus actually brings to a sharp definition the very paradigm of destruction and re-creation that the Hebrew Bible enshrined. If there is an ethic-dogmatic core at work, it is the affirmation of the steadfastness of God's creative love, which calls for imitation on the part of God's creatures. Categorically rejected is a theology based on retributive justice, which is seen as the product of those who believe that they know better than God and who cave in to the power of evil that keeps creeping into the cosmic order.

The strategic maneuver has an even broader encompassing goal. By changing the order of the books in the Septuagint and placing, at the end of the collection, the book of Malachi, which emphasizes expectation of the coming of the messiah, the early church vitiated the transition to the Christian Testament. But more significant is what this new ordering replaces. The Hebrew Bible ends with 2 Chronicles, and its last verses, far from stressing messianic expectation, lift up a Gentile, Cyrus, the Persian king, who issues an edict providing for a place of worship in Jerusalem where all of God's people can gather in pilgrimage. This conviviality of different religions, as seen in Cyrus' edict, does not imply conversion or supersession but rather affirms the diversity that God has intended from the onset of creation. Implied in this vision is the peaceful coexistence of a plurality of religious expressions—languages through which humans may carry on their conversation with and about God. This book invites the reader to enter the world of the Bible and join this conversation.

Vítor Westhelle

Acknowledgments

I would like to thank my brother, Dr. Bruce A. Butterfield, for his insightful criticism and attention to detail in editing the manuscript.

Introduction

THE AIM OF THIS little book is to give the general reader an up-to-date and understandable reading of the Hebrew Bible. Our interpretation will certainly have spillover effects on readings of the New Testament, too, and we will be sure to explain those effects.

Whatever else one may think about the Hebrew Bible, it is widely regarded as great literature. In fact, the Hebrew Bible is often credited with defining what it means to be human. Like all great literature, it tells stories not because the events described actually happened that way, but because they should have happened that way in order for the story to be effective politically or to suggest something insightful about humans or God. This fact may be unsettling for those who have been reading the Hebrew Bible as if it were a history book, but the Hebrew Bible has no interest in history in the modern sense of factually accurate reporting. Instead, the Hebrew Bible reshapes historical events as necessary or even invents them for the sake of storytelling. But it's important to understand that the value of the Hebrew Bible is not determined by its factual accuracy any more than the value of *Hamlet* depends on whether there actually was a Danish prince by that name. If the Hebrew Bible's value to us depended on its factual accuracy, then it would lose its value as soon as factual errors were discovered. All of this applies equally well to the New Testament, which is also Jewish literature, even if it is not part of normative Judaism.

Making Sense of the Hebrew Bible

It is also important to realize that the Hebrew Bible was not written for the reading pleasure of us moderns. Texts were composed, edited, and made public out of the need to respond to real-life historical situations. We cannot expect to appreciate these texts unless we understand the situations to which they are responding. To understand those situations, we will make use of the latest archaeological evidence.

One of the problems we face in reflecting on the Hebrew Bible is that it is notoriously complex, with a wide variety of contributions from different social groups at different moments in Israel's history. A further problem is that the Hebrew Bible, like other great literature, is metaphorical and does not offer any summaries or explicitly tell the reader what it is trying to say. For all these reasons, the Hebrew Bible can easily be misinterpreted and misused. To help overcome this difficulty, we will search for the Hebrew Bible's literary structure and for the theology that depends on that structure. Texts that either strongly support that theology or strongly oppose it can be thought of as crucial for our understanding of the whole. This is a way of allowing the Hebrew Bible itself to identify what's important in its vast collection of texts. Since these texts respond to real-life situations, we will often have to talk about what actually happened in Israel—not only what the Hebrew Bible chooses to say about Israelite history.

We will make an effort to keep this discussion as jargon-free as possible. We will argue solely on the basis of data that are well known and widely accepted by biblical archaeologists and biblical scholars both Jewish and Christian. So then, let's begin at the beginning.

1

In the Beginning

SINCE THE FIRST TEXT in the Hebrew Bible can be thought of as setting the stage for what follows and announcing what the whole collection is about, we will begin our study with Gen 1:1—2:4a. This text is known as a creation story, and it certainly is in the sense that it emphasizes that the God of Israel is the Creator. But it is not a story about the "how" of creation or about how long creation took. The following discussion takes Claus Westermann's *Creation* as its point of departure. Our intent is to explore the implications of his study.

When the biblical text says that God created by speaking, it admits that the process of creation remains a total mystery.[1] Hence, this story does not in any way pretend to be a scientific theory. Instead, it tries to describe something important that lies outside the realm of science—namely, the relationships that ought to exist among nature, humans, and God. Notice that we said "ought" because the priestly author of this text, writing shortly after the Babylonian exile, understood very well that, in the world he knew, those relationships were distorted and perverted. Since this story comes first in the Hebrew Bible and serves to introduce all that follows, we should recognize that what the Hebrew Bible implies it is trying to do is to confront "what is" in the world with "what ought to be."

1. Westermann, *Creation*, 42, 48.

This story serves as a corrective to the extremely negative situation the author has witnessed, especially in Babylon. During the Babylonian exile (during the sixth century BCE) the author got firsthand experience of Babylonian culture, which he presumably found repulsive because it grossly disrespected human dignity. In Babylonian religion, the stars, planets, sun, and moon were all deities, and those deities were pictured as violent and unfriendly to humans. The basic purpose of Babylonian religion was apparently to manipulate the common people through fear and convince them that it was the will of the gods that ordinary Babylonians should be content with their role as agricultural slaves.[2] The Babylonian creation myth, in fact, describes human beings as having been created as an afterthought and solely for the purpose of growing food for the gods. It is in reaction against this rather demeaning theological anthropology that the Hebrew author tells his fellow Israelites—and anyone else who will listen—how humans and the rest of nature ought to be understood. The fact that the editors of the Hebrew Bible put this text at the head of the collection is quite meaningful. It means that the Hebrew Bible introduces itself by saying that it constitutes a protest by an oppressed people who boldly denounce false gods and demeaning theological anthropologies while proclaiming the one true God and explaining how things ought to be in this world.

This creation story (Gen 1:1—2:4a) begins with God's imposing order upon the waters, which—importantly—are known in ancient mythology as the abode of the chaos monster Mot (Death). Thus, it is immediately clear that this story celebrates life and God's sovereignty, especially over the forces of evil. Then, after lampooning Babylonian religion by de-deifying the stars, the sun, the moon, and the planets and thus rendering them benign,[3] the author goes on to describe the awe-inspiring abundance, complexity, diversity, and constant growth of the natural world, which God

---

2. For more on this view of the Babylonian creation myth, see Hyers, *Meaning of Creation*.

3. Westermann, *Creation*, 44.

blesses and finds to be good and which the reader is thereby also encouraged to find good.

Eventually (Gen 1:26), the author is ready to talk about human beings. He tells us that all human beings, women and men alike, are created to be very much like God—so much like God, in fact, that God finds it appropriate to delegate to human beings responsibility for caring for what God has created. Note also that in this text humans receive the same blessing as the animals, a fact meant to remind us that however brilliant and important we may be as a species, we are still part of the earth's fauna. In any case, this divine delegation of authority to humans represents the noblest affirmation ever made of the value and dignity of human life and human agency. If we believe in the value of human life and in our responsibility to conserve and protect the environment, we should know that we owe these ideals to Gen 1:1—2:4a. The text emphasizes our dignity and our responsibility in two ways: (1) it describes us as made in God's own image and likeness; and (2) in order to say that we "have dominion" over nature, it uses the Hebrew verb *radah*, which throughout the rest of the Hebrew Bible is used only in reference to God. This important fact not only emphasizes the unique and privileged character of this delegation of authority and responsibility, but also implies that our dominion over nature must reflect God's own intelligence and love.[4]

It is important to note that God delegates this authority and responsibility to every member of the human species, not only to some elite class of people. This means that all human beings have both God-given dignity and a responsibility to protect the dignity of every member of our species, not only the members of a certain class, race, clan, tribe, sect, club, or nation. In other words, the task God assigns to us demands that we be radically and inclusively altruistic, and that altruism is to be understood as a powerful antidote to the oppression and exploitation the author has witnessed in Babylon. Hence, this text's statement about human responsibility and human dignity is both a protest against the way things are in the world and a bold declaration of the way they ought to be.

4. Ibid., 52.

What is not so obvious in this text is that, since God acts alone as the Creator, God must surely be lonely. God's intentional choice to create us to be very much like God implies that God wants us to relieve his/her loneliness by being God's conversation partners. Therefore, in carrying out the responsibilities God has assigned to us, we are naturally expected to remain in close communication with God. Contrary to Babylonian religion, we humans are not dull, mindless manpower; we are deeply spiritual creatures inspired and informed by the Creator God and meant to be friends and partners with God. This is a sublime vision of what it means to be human. Our being made in the image and after the likeness of God is a metaphorical way of saying that we are extremely well suited for this role.

What more can be said about us human beings? First, while the Babylonians were taught by their religion to fear and distrust nature, this text teaches us implicitly to love it, study it, understand it, and care for it wisely. Given the complexity of everything in nature—especially living organisms and the ecosystems in which they live—it is extraordinarily difficult for us to understand nature and manage it wisely. We humans must therefore have the most extraordinary intellect and intellectual curiosity. That is what this text implies.

We might pause here to ask why it is, for example, that we moderns believe so strongly in education. Is it only because education is necessary for getting a job or maintaining a democracy? Or is it also because we believe that every member of the human species is gifted with intelligence and intellectual curiosity, which must be nurtured and developed? This latter idea, as modern as it may seem, comes implicitly from Gen 1:1—2:4a.

This text also implies that since we humans are charged with defending the dignity of every member of our species, we must necessarily have a great sensitivity to questions of justice. In order for us to be God's agents on earth we must be endowed with justice sensitivity. And don't we know from our experience that we can in fact recognize injustice when we see it and that we have a visceral reaction to it? Almost any example of injustice offends us, and we are even more offended if the perpetrator is a person with power and the victim is weak and innocent. The task God assigns to us requires exercising our justice sensitivity so as to correct injustice and defend the dignity of every member of our species. Thus, contrary to Babylonian religion, we humans are not insensitive brutes fit only for hard labor. Because we are endowed with justice sensitivity, God can reasonably expect us to uphold justice and correct injustice just as God would do.

Even an atheist should recognize that this text correctly understands how we humans are constructed and is a brilliant and bold defense of human dignity. This dignity is in our DNA. It's a gift. It therefore doesn't have to be earned. But, importantly, it does have to be defended. If we believe in God, we may go one step further and understand that our full humanity expresses itself not only in our behavior relative to nature and to other humans but also in our spirituality. As agents of God on earth, we find our fullest humanity through conscious, intentional partnership with God as we go about conserving nature and defending justice and human dignity. Here we might add, parenthetically, that even though this story has no scientific pretensions, it is quite science-friendly in that it encourages and even requires studying both nature and humans.

This amazing story (Gen 1:1—2:4a) is divided into time sections (literally, days). The purpose of this temporal scheme is to show that creation is not static and not a one-time event but is instead active and ongoing and is headed somewhere. In the sixth time section, human beings are created. Then in the seventh section God refuses to work, having completed God's work in creation. The paradox found in Gen 2:2–3 is both amusing and significant. The text says that God has finished creating, but then, by refusing to work, God in effect creates rest. The verb this text uses to say that God refused to work is *shabat*, which literally means "he went on strike." God goes on strike and thus creates rest. The concept of rest is not new to us moderns, but it was strikingly new at the time this text was written. As mentioned above, Babylonian religion pictured humans as simply cheap labor. The serenely beautiful vision of this biblical text, however, is that, though we humans have much work to do—and this work can and should be hugely dignifying—we are meant for greater things than our work. Our final destination is to enjoy the leisure that God has created for the purpose of sharing it with us. And since we implicitly have, according to this story, a fiduciary responsibility toward animals, they too must have their leisure.

The implications of our intentional refusal to work are far-reaching. If we rest simply because we're tired, then we are doing something beneficial for our health but nothing more. If, however, one day out of every seven we intentionally refuse to work, we are expressing our value as human beings apart from our work and are protesting against the fact that many people are being exploited for their labor. At the same time, we are experiencing in advance the leisure God has promised as our destiny. Similarly, the reason people worship God on whatever day they designate as their Sabbath is that, according to the logic of this text, such worship celebrates in advance and even hastens the day when human beings will be fully at leisure with God. We might call that day the Great and Final Sabbath, which in this story can be thought of as the end-point of the creation process. Our refusal to work on the Sabbath promotes this process and constitutes participation in the life of God. And isn't such participation the whole point of our being created in the image and after the likeness of God? In fact, even an atheist can rest assured that he is doing something of great significance when once a week he refuses to work or to be defined solely by his work. By intentionally resting, the atheist is closer to God than he ever imagined he'd be or perhaps ever wanted to be.

As mentioned above, this creation story is organized according to a time sequence that has a beginning and an end point, and in that end point humans are destined to enjoy God's company and share in God's leisure. To more fully appreciate the practical significance of that sequence, we need to remember that in this story God is pictured as rather distant from what God has created. If we diagram the sentence, God the creator is the subject, and we the created are the object, with an unavoidable distance stretching between subject and object. But the text also tells us that God loves what God has created and that God loves us humans even more than God loves the rest of creation. The implication is that God must be suffering because of his separation from the whole created world and especially from us, his beloved conversation partners. The question for God is how to bridge the distance that separates God from us. God's solution to this problem, the text implies, lies within the very role God has assigned to us.

This role, as we have seen, consists in our doing what God would do if God were present in the created world and not distant from it. Thus, the implication of this text is that God expects somehow to be present in creation through our agency. Every time we act to play out our assigned role, God becomes at least briefly present among us. Curiously, even the most committed atheist may experience this phenomenon. For example, if we humans witness some real injustice, we have the undeniable feeling that we are involved in something much larger than ourselves. We feel deeply the seriousness of what we've witnessed, and there is no way we can ignore it or laugh it off. In fact, we have the feeling that this event somehow touches all humanity, and we may therefore even have the impression that we are somehow not alone in witnessing this injustice. And if we should attempt to undo the injustice, to right the wrong, we have the extraordinary sensation that we are somehow not acting alone either. This experience is not limited to people of faith because all humans are endowed with these justice sensitivities. This text encourages us to recognize, nurture, and act upon those sensitivities.

This same possibility for experiencing the presence of God is found in every aspect of the role God has given us. God becomes present in us and among us, and we become more socially and spiritually evolved when we put our whole selves into playing out our role. The lamentable fact, however, is that we humans tend to be rather uncommitted and inconsistent in playing our role, and as a result God can be only sporadically present among us. At this point in the discussion, though, we should be able to better understand the significance of the Great and Final Sabbath talked about earlier. It's that moment in time when we have played our role so well that God's presence among us is no longer occasional or sporadic but regular and consistent. Such is the goal of creation, the point at which we will have become fully human and at which God finally will be fully among us and thus feel loved and be happy.

The Hebrew Bible asserts in many ways that what most characterizes God is steadfast love (*hesed*). Now we can see what that term means. It means that God commits to being the partner of humans. How so? If God cannot escape loneliness and cannot be fully God, except through our actions, God is linking God's own well-being to ours, so that we can't talk about God's happiness without talking about our own and vice versa. This divine love is steadfast in the sense that God never gives up on us, never stops trying to get us to love God in return.

In conclusion, Gen 1:1—2:4a is first of all a daring protest story, and a very ambitious protest, too, in the sense that it offers a brilliant alternative to what it protests against. This alternative vision teaches us what it means to be truly human and at the same time says something important about what it means to be God. In this way, the protest story subtly morphs into a love story in which a lonely and loving God invites us to act in ways that, besides protecting and respecting nature, lead to our becoming more fully human and give God a chance to share our company and be happy.

It should be obvious that, regardless of one's faith or unfaith, this text is extremely valuable. It tells us who we human beings really are and what we are supposed to be doing in relation both to the natural environment and to other humans.

Besides benefitting both nature and God, the invitation or delegation God gives us in this text is clearly in our own best interests. But we humans, despite our amazing talents—or perhaps because of them—seem strangely reluctant to accept God's invitation and curiously incapable of recognizing what's good for us or for the environment. Another peculiar aspect of the human situation is that we humans may actually want to play the role God has assigned to us but find ourselves somehow blocked, psychologically or otherwise.

The whole rest of the Hebrew Bible and the New Testament, too, reveal what God does to overcome those impediments.

Continuing our discussion, we should bear in mind that the Hebrew Bible is metaphorical rather than historical. If its texts were historical, their significance would be limited to their specific moment in history. But since they are metaphorical, their truth can be applied to analogous situations at any time and in any place.

2

Stringing Stories Together with Metaphors

WE HAVE JUST SEEN that in Gen 1:1—2:4a God remains at some distance from human beings but that God truly cares for us humans and of course wants to interact with us. The account of those interactions begins with Adam and Eve. Yes, they are the first human beings but only in the sense that someone had to appear first in this story. In fact, Adam and Eve are simply representative human beings, and they qualify as representative because they are very intelligent and know it, and their self-awareness leads them to think that God has made a mistake in forbidding them to eat of the tree of knowledge and that, in this case at least, they know better than God. They quickly learn that their attitude is not pleasing to God or helpful to themselves, but, contrary to what so many Christian theologians have assumed, Adam and Eve's self-deception and resulting disobedience (the exact nature of which we can safely ignore in this discussion) are not some sort of breach in the dike that lets in the tsunami of all subsequent human disobedience. Adam and Eve are simply parade examples of what God usually encounters in dealing with us humans. Note that God in no way gives up on Adam and Eve in spite of their bad decision. Instead God acts to protect them by making clothes for them and making sure they can't get back into the garden and harm themselves further. Moreover God continues to believe that humans can actually do the right thing. We see good evidence of God's optimism in God's assurances that Cain is quite capable of overcoming his evil tendency (Gen 4:6–7). Unfortunately Cain proves resistant to instruction and kills his brother Abel anyway, and both Cain's attitude and the murder he commits are a foretaste of the human errors to come in the story.

As the human population in this story grows, it also becomes increasingly disobedient and violent. God concludes that these humans are simply incorrigible and regrets having created them. Despite God's demonstrated love for humans—or perhaps precisely because of it—God sends a flood to destroy this corrupt humanity, except for the good man Noah and his family, so that God can re-create the world after the flood by means of the sons of Noah. But this plan doesn't work out so well either because, before long, the post-flood humans disobey God by trying to destroy the diversity that God loves so much. In particular, they want all people to speak the same language (Gen 11), although such homogenization defies God's intentions in creation. As we saw in Gen 1:1—2:4a and can readily observe in nature and in human society, God loves diversity. There is, after all, enormous diversity not only in plant and animal species but in human cultures, races, languages, and religions. God doesn't want everyone to look the same, speak the same language or have the same culture or religion; God loves diversity.

At this point in the narrative God makes an important decision: to stop addressing humanity as one big group. Apparently the problem is class size. Too many students were crowded into God's classroom, and it proved unmanageable. So God chooses to address humanity in a new way: by selecting and training a small group who will love and obey God, grow into a great people, teach others by example, and thus be a blessing to all humankind. For this purpose God chooses Abram, a descendant of Shem, one of Noah's sons. Abram and his wife, Sarai, will be the building blocks of this training group, which will grow and eventually be called Israel.

But remember that none of this is historical. The biblical authors are not telling us what actually happened; they are creating narratives that give some flavor of God's experiences first with humans in general and then with the people who eventually became Israel. The stories about Abraham, Isaac, Jacob, and Joseph are similarly unhistorical. These figures are best understood as metaphorical ancestors of the people of Israel. Scholars have for the past fifty years suspected that these stories were written long after the events described, and there is now good reason for thinking that these narratives were composed in the seventh century BCE during the reign of King Josiah for the purpose of promoting his reform.[1]

What the patriarchal narratives (Gen 12–50) do is to introduce the very important idea of God's covenant with Israel. According to this covenant, God will, in exchange for Israel's loyalty to God above all things, make Israel into a great nation residing on its own land. The story of God's fulfilling this covenant and of Israel's learning to be loyal to God alone is told in such a way as to provide some plausible, if largely invented, background for the idea that the people of Israel are one family. Conveying that single idea may have been the immediate purpose of these narratives for Josiah's reform. But the value of these narratives goes far beyond the simple notion of the basic unity of Israel. The patriarchal narratives are sophisticated literature built upon the most subtle and nuanced interconnections.[2] But, for the purposes of our study, we need to understand at least the basics of these narratives.

Let us begin with Exod 22:28-29, the text that clearly describes the stringent test that God uses to assess Israel's loyalty. God says, "You shall not put off the skimming of the first yield of your vats. You shall give me the firstborn among your sons. You shall do the same with your cattle and your flocks: seven days it shall remain with its mother; on the eighth day you shall give it to me."

For most modern readers, the sacrifice of animals is repugnant, and the sacrifice of a son is even more abhorrent. But the sacrifice of a son did not become generally abhorrent in Israel until

---

1. For more on this subject, see Finkelstein and Silberman, *Bible Unearthed*, 27-47.

2. Anyone desiring to appreciate these narratives in all their brilliant details should see Levenson, *Death and Resurrection*, 1-199.

the time of Jeremiah and Ezekiel (sixth century BCE), who both railed against it.[3] Until that time, however, child sacrifice was not unusual in Israel. But it is important to realize that this practice had redemptive purposes, a fact clearly stated much later in the New Testament in John 3:16: "For God so loved the world that he gave his only Son." Importantly, the Gospel of John uses the same verb "give/gave" that is traditionally associated with sacrifice.[4] In other words, the practice of child sacrifice may have died out, but the theology of child sacrifice continued to be very influential for both Jews and Christians, as seen also in the fact that both venerate Abraham for his willingness to sacrifice his son Isaac.

It is fascinating that, although Exod 22:28-29 calls for the sacrifice of firstborn sons, none of the sons who are important in God's fulfilling of his covenant with Israel are firstborn sons. This remarkable deviation from the expected begins in Exod 4, where Eve gives birth first to Cain and then Abel. Thus Cain is the firstborn son, but, importantly, God favors Abel. God's preference is arbitrary and has no logical explanation.[5] Thus it is far more important to be the favored son than simply the firstborn. When Abel is killed, we become aware of the awful consequences associated with being the favored son: as the favored son, he is exalted but also humiliated/killed.

In Exod 4, we also find two genealogies: one for the line of Cain, which quickly dies out, and another for the line of Eve's third son, Seth, from whom all humanity descends. Thus Seth is Abel *redivivus* and receives the blessing and status that Abel should have received, so that Seth reveals the fuller pattern of the favored son: exaltation, simultaneous humiliation, and then exaltation once again.[6] It is this fuller pattern that the New Testament writers find in the death and resurrection of Jesus Christ, as most clearly expressed in Phil 2:1-11.

3. Ibid., 4-6.
4. Ibid., 31.
5. Ibid., 72-74.
6. Ibid., 78.

At the end of Exod 11, we learn that Abram, who is later to become Abraham, has a nephew named Lot, who is already an adult. Yet in Exod 12, God favors the already old man Abram over the younger man Lot, who would have been the logical choice for the assignment God gives to Abram. But it is more important to be favored by God than to be the logical man for the job. Abram receives God's promise that he will become the father of a great people through whom all the nations will be blessed; he also receives many material benefits. But then he and his wife Sarai have to flee to Egypt, where they are both humiliated. Abram is supposed to become the father of a great people, but Sarai is sterile. When she is unable to become pregnant, she encourages Abram to father a child by her maidservant, Hagar. The plan works, and Hagar gives birth to Ishmael, who is thus Abram's firstborn son. But God does not favor Ishmael and insists upon waiting for Sarai to conceive. As a sign of promise, God changes Abram's name to Abraham and Sarai's name to Sarah (Exod 17). Then by divine intervention Sarah finally conceives and gives birth to Isaac, who is a second son but the one whom God favors. When Isaac is an adolescent, God commands Abraham to sacrifice his son, his only son, who represents an indispensable part of the fulfillment of God's promises to Abraham. Thus this command severely tests Abraham's willingness to put loyalty to God above every competitor.[7] Abraham must be willing to sacrifice Isaac, who not only is his own child but now plays the role of the favored son, both exalted and simultaneously humiliated. Once Abraham demonstrates his radical trust in God, God intervenes, so that Isaac does not have to die.

When Isaac grows up, he marries Rebekah, who gives birth first to Esau and then Jacob. But God favors Jacob. Thus we might even say that it is God's will that Jacob swindle Esau out of his birthright and his blessing. Because of this swindle, Jacob—not Esau—becomes heir to the line of Abraham, but, as the favored son, Jacob is simultaneously humiliated by being alienated from his brother and exiled. In exile he falls in love with Rachel, but her father, Laban, tricks Jacob into first marrying Rachel's older

---

7. Ibid., 125–28.

sister, Leah: the conman gets conned. Thus the favored son is both exalted and repeatedly humiliated.

Jacob has many sons with Leah, whom he does not love, and other sons with maid servants, but Rachel, whom he really loves, is childless for a long time until finally giving birth to Joseph and Benjamin. One day while most of Jacob's sons are out in the pasture with their sheep, he gives Joseph a fancy coat that indicates that Joseph is the favored son and heir. As soon as his older brothers see Joseph in that coat, they want to kill him. One of the brothers convinces them to sell Joseph into slavery instead. As favored son and heir, he is exalted. Then he is immediately humiliated by being sold into Egypt. There he rises to a position of eminence from which he is able to rescue all Israel, and he is thus exalted once again.

The patriarchs are all second or late-born sons, whom God, defying convention, favors as the recipients of his covenant promises. Of all these examples, the most complete and satisfying is that of Joseph, who makes the full circuit from exalted to humiliated to exalted again.

At the same time as these favored sons are being simultaneously exalted and humiliated, they are also being transformed in a process of destruction followed by re-creation. For example, at the end of Gen 11, Abram, who is fond of his house, his city, his extended family, and his sedentary lifestyle, is in the next chapter completely transformed and replaced by a wildly adventurous Abram who sets out for places unknown on the apparently impossible mission of becoming the father of a great nation, even though he and his sterile wife are already old. Because Abram has trusted God's promises, God changes Abram's name, and then tests him in the most radical way by commanding him to sacrifice his son Isaac. By means of this test, the Abraham who had doubts about whether God's promises could actually be realized is destroyed, so to speak, and replaced by the Abraham who trusts God implicitly. The same is true of Isaac, who also is tested alongside his father. Isaac is old enough to know that his father has every intention of sacrificing him, but Isaac remains radically obedient to God throughout the ordeal and emerges ready to assume his role as rightful heir to God's covenant promises. Jacob undergoes a similar change. At the River Jabbok (Exod 32), he wrestles with the angel of God—a near-death experience—and, as a result, the swindler Jacob is transformed and replaced by the faithful and honest Jacob, his transformation marked by the change of his name to Israel. In this way, the motif of the favored son, simultaneously exalted and humiliated, works in partnership with the motif of destruction and re-creation.

For the flow of this story, it's important that the Israelites eventually find themselves in Egypt. The Joseph story serves to transport them from Canaan to Egypt. Scholars now believe that the whole idea of the Israelites' being enslaved in Egypt and then liberated by God is a literary invention from the time of King Josiah, who at a certain point goes out to do battle with the pharaoh Necho. In this line of thinking, the Exodus narrative reflects the hope that God will be Josiah's liberator.[8] In any case, the exodus soon takes center stage, and Abraham, Isaac, and Jacob quickly fade into the background. They have their personality disorders, engage in much trickery and squabbling, and are troubled by all sorts of doubts and fears, but in the final analysis they reveal themselves to be radically obedient to God and eminently teachable. Thus nothing in them or in their experience constitutes an overwhelming obstacle to God's plan of making Israel into an exemplary and numerous people through whom all the nations will be blessed.

Such is not the case, however, when the Israelites find themselves enslaved in Egypt. As we learned in chapter 1, God loves us humans and naturally wants to be loved in return, and God is in fact loved in return by Abraham, Isaac, Jacob, and Joseph. But these characters are able to love God because they are free to love. Love by its very nature cannot be coerced; it has to be a free act, or it simply isn't love. A slave is not free to love—or to do anything else. Therefore, if the Israelites remained enslaved in Egypt, God's desire to be loved by them would be thwarted. Human dignity is

---

8. Finkelstein and Silberman, *Bible Unearthed*, 47–81.

also at stake. On the basis of Gen 1:1—2:4a, we know that God is intent on protecting and preserving human dignity. Thus, if God did not rescue the Israelites from slavery in Egypt, God's plans for Israel and for humans in general would definitely be stalled. But, even more importantly, God must rescue the Israelites from Egypt in order to be faithful to the covenant promises that God made to the patriarchs.

Now it's true, as we will see more fully in chapter 3, that the archaeological evidence tells us that in all probability the Israelites were never as a group enslaved in Egypt and that there never was an exodus such as the one described in the book of Exodus. But that fact only makes the Exodus narrative all the greater as a literary achievement. Any good journalist can write a reasonably accurate report of what actually happened in any particular event, but only a religious and literary genius could write a story about an exodus that never happened and make that story so deeply insightful, moving, and true in what it says about God and humans that we are still talking about it thousands of years later. The metaphor of exodus and the rebirth it makes possible is so powerful in fact that it is applied repeatedly in the Hebrew Bible and in the New Testament and for millennia has played a major role for both Jews and Christians. In fact, the Exodus narrative is in the view of most scholars the single most useful text in either the Hebrew Bible or the New Testament.

What makes the Exodus narrative so useful? It's mainly that the metaphor of liberation from slavery is so flexible that it can be applied to all sorts of situations in which people would like to respond positively to God's love but are somehow impeded or blocked. Even today there are many people who are literally enslaved and who very much need to be physically liberated, but there are even more people whose bonds are less visible and who do not necessarily appear to need liberation—but in fact do. Many forces bind people and prevent them from loving God in return, yet the exodus metaphor fits every such situation. For this reason reading the Exodus narrative can be a profoundly moving experience, which, like some other experiences mentioned above, is universal.

It knows no racial, ethnic, or religious boundaries because everyone has experienced or still needs some form of liberation.

The power of the Exodus narrative is especially great for people who have done a lot of living and so have a history of psychological or physical enslavement, catastrophe, or disappointment. People who identify with the Israelites' being set free from bondage in Egypt are better able to face the problems in their own lives or in the life of their community. They remember how absolutely devastated they once felt, how bleak their prospects were, but also how they or their community survived nonetheless. Even the most pampered and uneventful life has its share of catastrophes real or imagined, and when we think honestly about our own, we acknowledge that we didn't rescue ourselves. We know that we had help, and we want to give thanks. This is true for people of faith in God and for others, too.

Another conclusion we may draw when we read the Exodus narrative is that, if we ourselves or our community have needed to be liberated and rescued again and again, many other people must need liberation and rescue, too. And since God has delegated to us the responsibility of doing on earth what God would do, we need to be thinking about ways to liberate these people.

In the ancient Near East, slavery, forced labor, indentured servitude, and oppression were common. If Finkelstein and Silberman are correct,[9] the author of the Exodus narrative was thinking only of Josiah's conflict with Necho and Judah's desire to be free from Egyptian interference and oppression. But we can now recognize that, in the process of telling the exodus story, the author effectively invents the whole concept of liberation. More than that, the author gives the credit for liberation to the God of Israel, and that attribution was quite revolutionary because in the ancient Near East, anyone powerful enough to enslave another person must have had a stronger god. But in the case of the Israelites, who were very weak, their God shows himself/herself to be more powerful than the gods of the Egyptian slave masters. The

---

9. Ibid., 275–79.

Stringing Stories Together with Metaphors

revolutionary message is that false gods enslave, but that the God of Israel liberates.

God's agent in the exodus was of course Moses. In the opening chapters of the book of Exodus we find the story of the Israelite mother of the baby Moses casting him adrift on the Nile in a watertight basket and of the pharaoh's daughter picking him up out of the basket and raising him in her father's court. This is a lovely story all by itself, as are the story of creation, the story of Noah and his ark, and especially the story of the exodus. Each one of these is a literary gem in its own right. But something else is going on here, something absolutely brilliant and marvelous, which is recognizable only in the Hebrew-language text. The editor of these texts found a way to use imagery to connect these originally separate stories so that, linked together, their power is greatly magnified. Let's see how that is done.

In the first creation story (Gen 1:9) God separates the oceans from the dry land—a separation that creates the habitat that makes human life possible and helps account for the abundance of species of both flora and fauna. The separation of the land from the waters is thus a key step in creation. Then, in the Noah story (Gen 8:13), after the great flood the waters are separated from the dry land, and life begins again. The world is re-created. In the story of Moses's birth, the baby Moses is separated from the waters thanks to the watertight basket and then is further rescued from the waters by Pharaoh's daughter. In the exodus story the ocean waters are separated from the dry land (Exod 14:21–22) so that a long, narrow passage—a sort of birth canal—opens up for the Israelites as they flee from the pursuing Egyptian army. When the Israelites reach the other end of this passage, they are effectively reborn: no longer enslaved but free. And just to make sure that the reader of the Hebrew text does not miss these connections, the biblical editor uses the same noun *tayvah* for both Noah's ark and the watertight basket used by Moses' mother. In literature nothing is accidental, and this detail certainly is not either. The idea is that just as Noah was key to God's plan of saving and re-creating human life, so Moses is essential to God's plan of saving and re-creating Israel—and, through Israel, all humankind.

We should mention that the rabbis have always insisted that God, who is quite sensitive to human suffering and loves all humans very much, was saddened by the fact that in order to liberate the Israelites, some Egyptians had to die. God took no pleasure at all in the death of the Egyptians even though they were in this case Israel's enemies—perhaps a lesson for us who are trying to be God's agents on earth.

What we have just seen in this discussion of separation from water is that the biblical editor uses creation imagery to talk about liberation, so that liberation results in re-creation: the old is destroyed (e.g., slavery), and something new is born (freedom). This linkage between creation imagery and liberation is so effective and so powerful that it is also used by the biblical authors to describe the return of the exiles from Babylonian captivity (late sixth century). When the exiles finally are permitted to leave Babylon and set out for Jerusalem, God pushes back the sands of the desert and opens a highway for the Israelites (Isa 40:3–5) much as the ocean waters are pushed back in the Exodus narrative, which describes events that are supposedly much earlier in Israel's history. This same creation-liberation imagery, which links the destruction of something moribund and enslaving with the creation of something new and liberating that needs to be born, is pervasive in the Hebrew Bible and also in the New Testament. Christians even participate in a liturgical drama that acts out this imagery. It's called baptism. Without this destruction/re-creation imagery the Passover *seder* would be just another congregational dinner, and without this imagery Jesus' death and resurrection wouldn't make much sense either.

We said earlier that we would let the Hebrew Bible tell us in its own way—that is, implicitly—what the most important texts are, and we have done that. We have discovered that the crucial moments in Israel's experience with God are described with destruction/re-creation imagery, and clearly, without this same imagery—with all of the implications discussed so far—the New Testament would lose much of its meaning, too. It is safe to

Stringing Stories Together with Metaphors

conclude, therefore, that we have found an idea that is fundamentally important to the Hebrew Bible and to the New Testament. That idea, simply put, is the following: whenever some obstacle blocks the ability or willingness of human beings, especially Israel, to love God, God does not hesitate to attempt to overcome that obstacle by performing a destruction followed by a re-creation. This same imagery remains very much alive in the life and discourse of both the synagogue and the church, and clearly such imagery has lost none of its explanatory power.

In chapter 1, we talked about creation as an ongoing process moving toward the Great and Final Sabbath. That process gets stalled with Adam and Eve, and then, in spite of the good man Noah, it gets completely derailed in the violence and confusion described in Gen 4–11. When God chooses Abram, however, things immediately improve, and, as we have already seen, Abraham, Isaac, and Jacob go through a process of more or less constant, though painful, transformation/re-creation until they have learned to love and trust God above every competitor.

We have also seen that the case of the Israelites in bondage in Egypt is a far more threatening situation than anything God faced with the patriarchs. Therefore God must resort to an even more drastic solution, such as in the time of Noah. Why does the Egyptian bondage require such a powerful and dramatic solution? It's because no matter how much you ameliorate slavery, it's still slavery until you destroy it. Very much the same can be said later when the Israelites who were liberated from slavery demonstrate in the wilderness wandering their incorrigible stubbornness: they have been physically liberated, but they refuse to be spiritually liberated. Thus there is nothing more God can do with them, except to resort to the drastic measure of preventing that generation of Israelites from entering the promised land. They must die in the desert, and only Israelites born during the wilderness wandering are permitted to enter. Or later (early sixth century BCE), when the Babylonians invade Judah and destroy the temple, a few prophets understand that the Babylonians are God's instruments for carrying out God's first step, namely, the destruction. Then, once the Israelites in exile have thoroughly repented, God takes care of the second step, namely, the re-creation. We learn from this that when God does a re-creation, it involves much more than tweaking the system; it means a gut-wrenching eradication of the old system and the creation of a new one. The psalmist in Ps 51, praying for God's forgiveness for horrendous sins, does not ask God to repair the old system; he pleads for a whole new system: destruction/re-creation. The editors of the Hebrew Bible choose to characterize Israel's history (and all human history) as a series of these destruction–re-creation cycles, and the authors of the New Testament have a similar understanding. That's why in the New Testament the sinner has to die to sin in order to be reborn. It's also why Jesus, who takes human sin upon himself, has to die rather than simply retire to the Galilee. There's no re-creation without destruction. Thus it is a mistake to blame anyone for Jesus' death. The destruction/re-creation paradigm runs all the way through the Hebrew Bible and the New Testament, and carried to its logical conclusion, it requires Jesus' death. It's what you might call a metaphorical necessity.

It's important to realize that the truth of this destruction/re-creation paradigm has applications far beyond biblical texts or things ordinarily thought of as religious. Take the case of alcoholics, for example. The only effective treatment for them is to die to their old self, their old life, if they expect to have a new life. This may very well also be true for vices, addictions, perversions, obsessions, or serious diseases: you can't recover by taking palliatives. The situation calls for destruction/re-creation. The biblical authors find this fact to have such fundamental importance that it becomes the paradigm for all of Israel's life with God.

Continuing our discussion, some readers may already know a great deal about the history of Israel, but if they studied that history by reading the Bible itself or any of the conventional histories of Israel, such as the famous one by John Bright, they definitely need an update. In the last thirty years much has changed in our knowledge about the history of Israel, and that will be the subject of our next chapter.

3

Israel's Real History

THOSE OF YOU WHO thought that the history of Israel is more or less the same as that described in the Hebrew Bible are certainly not alone. Until just fifteen or twenty years ago, most scholars assumed that the Hebrew Bible's own account, with exception made for the usual Near Eastern hyperbole, was historically reliable. Scholars felt comfortable in making that assumption because for the previous several hundred years the brightest and best theologian-archaeologists had tried very hard to assure biblical scholars of the Hebrew Bible's historical accuracy, and, in the absence of contradictory evidence, no one had reason to question that assurance. More recently, however, a new generation of archaeologists, with no particular theological axe to grind, have convincingly disproved the traditional claims for the Hebrew Bible's historicity. Finkelstein and Silberman's *The Bible Unearthed* is particularly helpful in explaining the newly discovered but by now widely acknowledged facts of Israel's history. By analyzing vast amounts of archaeological data and the theories that emerged from them, these authors present a detailed and carefully reasoned picture of Israel's real history and explain when and why a large part of the Hebrew Bible was produced. What follows summarizes and comments on their main arguments. This summary contains valuable information that every student of the Hebrew Bible should know, and we can't talk seriously about when and why biblical texts were produced without being clear about Israel's real history. We begin this summary of Finkelstein and Silberman with the so-called patriarchs: Abraham, Isaac, and Jacob, who supposedly existed in the early second millennium BCE.

The Archaeological Evidence according to Finkelstein and Silberman

The Patriarchs

Finkelstein and Silberman argue that, because of various telltale anachronisms, even if the patriarchal narratives contain some early traditions, their final composition dates from the eighth–seventh centuries BCE. The first of these anachronisms has to do with the patriarchal narratives' frequent references to camels (see Gen 37:25) and to the use of camels in the caravan trade. Camels were not domesticated until late in the second millennium and were not used in the caravan trade until well after 1000 BCE. Similarly, the products that the Joseph story says the camels carried are associated with the Arabian trade supervised by the Assyrians in the eighth–seventh centuries.

A second anachronism is the reference to the Philistines at the city of Gerar (Gen 26:1). The Philistines were not present in Canaan until after 1200 BCE, and Gerar (Gen 20:1) was, in the early phase of Philistine history, only a tiny village that did not become a real city until the eighth–seventh centuries.

The stories of Jacob's marriage with Leah and Rachel mention Arameans, but Arameans do not appear as a distinct ethnic group in the ancient Near East before 1100 BCE. The conflict between Jacob and Laban and their placement of a boundary stone to separate their peoples (Gen 31:45–55) reflects the situation of Aram and Israel in the ninth–eighth centuries. In the stories about Jacob and Esau, Jacob is the father of Israel, and Esau the father of Edom. But Edom didn't exist as a distinct political entity until the late eighth century BCE.

These and other anachronisms point to a composition date in the eighth and seventh centuries. Finkelstein and Silberman suggest that the patriarchal narratives should be thought of as a pious prehistory in which Judah played a decisive role—not surprising because by the late eighth and seventh centuries Judah was virtually all that was left of the Israelite nation. The purpose of these narratives was to redefine the unity of the people of Israel by picturing early Israel as the single family of Abraham, Isaac, and Jacob.

The Exodus

From the earliest recorded times, Semites immigrated to Egypt, especially to escape warfare, drought or famine, and independent archaeological and historical sources show that from time to time the Egyptians expelled these immigrants. The Egyptians were meticulous record-keepers, but they have no record of Israelite immigrants. Moreover, the Israelites did not emerge as a distinct group in Canaan until the beginning of the thirteenth century BCE, and there is no evidence of their being present in Egypt before that time.

Then there's the question of the means by which any group of people could escape from Egypt and go to Canaan. Through a whole series of forts, the Egyptians heavily patrolled and tightly controlled the border between Egypt and Canaan. If any group, particularly a large group, had attempted to flee from Egypt and enter Canaan, the Egyptians would have documented it. But no record exists. Moreover, in the thirteenth century BCE, Egypt was at the height of its power and exercised complete control over all of Canaan as well. The biblical narratives show an awareness of the danger of anyone's attempting to flee by the coastal route; hence the Israelites' decision (Gen 15:22) to turn toward the desolation of the Sinai Peninsula. But evidence for an Israelite presence in the Sinai does not exist. Modern archaeological techniques are capable of detecting even the smallest remains, and in fact remains of pastoral activity have been found in the Sinai for earlier and later periods. But there is no evidence of the exodus in the thirteenth century BCE. The conclusion

Finkelstein and Silberman draw is that the exodus did not happen at the time or in the way the Bible describes.

Instead, they argue, the Exodus narratives were composed in response to a growing conflict with Egypt in the seventh century BCE. The confrontation between Moses and the pharaoh was intended to prefigure the confrontation between King Josiah and the Pharaoh Necho. From this point of view, the Exodus narratives are best thought of as an expression of hope that God will defend and rescue Israel in its current conflict with Necho—and not as either historical truth or literary fiction.

Conquest of Canaan

Until recently most scholars believed that the Israelites conquered Canaan and that the conquest took place more or less as the Bible describes it. But that consensus has been abandoned for some or all of the following reasons:

1. At the time the conquest would have had to occur (the Late Bronze Age, 1550–1150 BCE), Canaan was an Egyptian province closely controlled by Egyptian administration and strongly defended by Egyptian garrisons throughout the country. It is highly unlikely that the Egyptians would have allowed anyone to disrupt or even destroy so many of their loyal vassal cities. Moreover, extensive Egyptian records show no trace of any such disruption or destruction.

2. The archaeological evidence regarding the cities of Canaan contradicts the biblical account. For example, the cities of Canaan were unfortified. Jericho not only had no walls but was uninhabited in the thirteenth century BCE. Prior to that time Jericho had been a small, poor, insignificant, unwalled settlement. Moreover, there is no sign of destruction at that site.

3. Much the same can be said for ancient Ai. Absolutely no sign of settlement in the Late Bronze Age has been found there.

4. As for Gibeon, remains have been found there from the Middle Bronze Age and from the Iron Age, but none from the Late Bronze Age.

5. The same holds true for other cities mentioned in the conquest narratives and in the summary list of the kings of Canaan (Joshua 12).

6. As for the destruction of Bethel, Lachish, Hazor, Megiddo, and Aphek, archaeological evidence shows that someone else—not the Israelites—was responsible. In any case, the destruction took place during more than a century and could not conceivably have been executed by a single military force and certainly not in one campaign.

The question is why the conquest narratives would describe this Late Bronze Age collapse not as what it actually was—namely, a chaotic series of upheavals with multiple causes involving multiple groups over a long period of time—but as a fast-moving conquest carried out with God's blessing and under God's direction.

The answer now widely accepted is that in the seventh century BCE, when the Assyrian empire collapsed and the Assyrians withdrew from Israel, the unification of all Israelites seemed possible. The conquest narratives present a vision of future territorial expansion, which was one of Josiah's dreams. The book of Joshua teaches an important and relevant lesson: when the people of Israel observe the torah, unification becomes possible. In this way the book of Joshua expresses the yearnings and fantasies of King Josiah. The figure of Joshua is thus a metaphorical prefiguration of Josiah.

The Question of Identity

There still remains the question of who these Israelites were. The answer has been slow in coming because most archaeological excavation in Israel has historically focused on the great Canaanite cities, such as Jericho, Bethel, Lachish, and Hazor. But those have turned out to be the wrong places to look for the origins of the Israelites. Fortunately, beginning in the 1940s, some archaeologists realized this mistake and undertook regional studies aimed at discovering settlement patterns over time. These studies produced revolutionary changes in the study of early Israel by discovering a densely grouped and complex network of villages in the central highlands of Canaan. Dramatic social transformation began there around 1200 BCE, but it did not involve violent invasion or even infiltration of any specific ethnic group. While the great Canaanite cities were in the process of collapse and disintegration, about 250 villages arose in the central hill country. These villages had no fortifications or weapons, and no signs of burning or violent attack could be found.

Finkelstein and Silberman say in conclusion:

> The process that we describe here is, in fact, the opposite of what we have in the Bible: the emergence of early Israel was an outcome of the collapse of the Canaanite culture, not its cause. And most of the Israelites did not come from outside Canaan—they emerged from within it. There was no mass exodus from Egypt. There was no violent conquest of Canaan. Most of the people who formed early Israel were local people—the same people whom we see in the highlands throughout the Bronze and Iron Ages. The early Israelites were—irony of ironies—themselves originally Canaanites![1]

Finkelstein and Silberman also say that there was no clear indication of what dialect was spoken in these highland villages or of what religious rituals, clothing, or burial practices people had.

So-Called United Kingdom

But what about the Davidic empire and the glories of King Solomon? On this question the archaeological evidence is negative, so that there is no reason to think that Jerusalem was a great city in the time of David or Solomon. The biblical description of the days of Solomon is an idealization. If David or Solomon had had any substantial wealth or power, it would be mentioned in some

1. Ibid., 118.

Egyptian or Mesopotamian text, but there is no such mention. Archaeological evidence for Solomon's famous building projects is nonexistent. But at least we know that David actually existed because the inscription of Mesha, king of Moab in the ninth century BCE, mentions David and thus validates him as the founder of a dynasty in Jerusalem.

According to Finkelstein and Silberman, the evidence very succinctly is as follows: (1) in the time of Saul (ca. 1025–1005), the Iron Age I settlement system continues in the highlands; (2) in the time of David (ca. 1005–970), there is no evidence for David's conquests or for his empire; in the highlands, the Iron Age I settlement system continues while Canaanite culture continues uninterrupted in the valleys; and (3) in the time of Solomon (ca. 970–931), there is no sign of monumental architecture; Jerusalem is not an important city; there is no sign of grand-scale building in Megiddo, Hazor, or Gezer; in the north, Canaanite culture continues. David and Solomon's homeland of Judah was very undeveloped, there being no evidence whatever that they had an empire at all, let alone a wealthy empire.

Reasons for Confusion about David and Solomon

Why, then, for so long did scholars actually believe in the vast extent of David's empire and in the grandeur of the Solomonic kingdom? The answer is that archaeologists misdated both "Davidic" and "Solomonic" remains by at least a century. In the tenth century Jerusalem and Judah were still remote and backward. But a century later they no longer were. It is for good political reasons that the Hebrew Bible imagines that David had an empire and that the Solomonic kingdom was glorious: these theological hopes were central to Josiah's vision of national renaissance. Such hopes could not be realized, however, unless the people of Israel, exhausted from much warfare and lacking a sense of national unity, could be persuaded to believe that in the time of David they had won great victories through divine intervention. For this reason, writers working in the time of King Josiah portrayed David as a conquering and unifying hero—which he certainly was not—in order to prefigure the sort of king that Josiah wanted to be. In fact, they did the same thing with both Moses and Joshua, who, though not historical figures, both serve to foreshadow Josiah.

Israelite Settlements in Canaan

Beginning sometime in the thirteenth century BCE, the Israelites formed two distinct highland entities engaged sometimes in agriculture, other times in pastoralism, and still other times in both. The northern entity (Israel) was always much more prosperous because it occupied better land. The southern entity (Judah) was poorer, weaker, and less influential. In the time of David, Solomon, and Rehoboam, Jerusalem was no more than a poor highland village and did not develop into a real city until after the fall of the northern kingdom of Israel (ca. 720 BCE). In fact, Judah did not become a state until then. The Hebrew Bible claims that Israel seceded from Judah, but that story is belied by the historical evidence. The Deuteronomistic historian (the author of Deuteronomy through 2 Kings), working in the time of Josiah, conveys a contradictory message about the northern kingdom. On the one hand, he pretends that the northern kingdom was part of the mythical united monarchy of David and Solomon; that its people were Israelites who should have pledged their loyalty to Jerusalem and worshiped there; and that Josiah, the heir to the Davidic throne, was the only legitimate heir to the territories of Israel. On the other hand, the Deuteronomistic historian demeans and delegitimizes the northern cult and replaces it with centralized worship at the Jerusalem temple. The reason for this is that the Deuteronomistic historian is trying to support Josiah's ambition to expand to the north and take over the territories of Israel now that the Assyrians have withdrawn (mid-seventh century BCE).

Beginnings of the Bible

As just mentioned, Israel was rich while Judah was poor. Israel was sufficiently wealthy and organized to enjoy literacy, a diversified economy, monumental building, a professional army, and a professional bureaucracy. Moreover, it had a complex system of cities, towns, and villages. Its character, politics, and religious practices differed markedly from those of Judah, which consisted only of impoverished villages where David and Solomon were really not kings at all but only village chieftains. As we've seen, the Hebrew Bible was largely composed during the reign of King Josiah of Judah (late seventh century BCE), and Josiah certainly did not want the Israelite kings, who profaned themselves by doing business with the nations (making deals with first Damascus and then Assyria), had foreign wives, and copied Canaanite architecture in their shrines and palaces, to be seen as rich and successful. As a result, the Deuteronomistic historian intentionally demeans and misrepresents the northern kingdom as part of his propaganda in favor of Josiah's territorial and religious ambitions.

Assyrian Invasion of Northern Kingdom

When the Assyrians conquered the northern kingdom, they carried out several deportations, but the total number of deportees was only about forty thousand people, and no more than a fifth of the population. Most of the surviving Israelites were left on the land, and the Assyrians had economic reasons for not devastating the rich agricultural area around the city of Samaria. The Assyrians destroyed the administrative centers but left the rural population unhurt. This population was Canaanite, Phoenician, and Aramean in tradition. These people lived alongside the new population brought in by the Assyrians. Meanwhile, as the northern kingdom was being conquered, Judah and Jerusalem were left untouched because they were too poor and inaccessible to be worth conquering.

South vs. North

The Deuteronomistic historian's treatment of the northern kingdom might make you think that Judah was religiously purer than Israel, but such is not the case. In the eighth century BCE, King Hezekiah of Judah carried out a sweeping religious reform, which the Deuteronomistic historian presents (2 Kgs 18:3–7) as a restoration of purity and fidelity to the God of Israel. But archaeology shows that the notion of a golden age of tribal and Davidic loyalty to the God of Israel was a late idealization, not a historical reality. Far from constituting a restoration, the idea of a centralized monarchy and of a national religion focused in Jerusalem was new in Hezekiah's time (late eighth and early seventh century BCE) since the people of Judah had been idol-worshipers for hundreds of years. The Deuteronomistic historian portrays King Ahaz, for example, as a notorious apostate who even burned his son as an offering (2 Kgs 16:2–4), but archaeology shows that there was nothing unusual about Ahaz. Such pagan practices were common in Judah and formed part of a set of rituals designed to appeal to various deities for fertility and well-being. Moreover, those practices are indistinguishable from those of neighboring peoples. Archaeology has found clay figurines, libation vessels, and offering stands throughout Judah, and those finds indicate that religious practices were highly varied, decentralized, and not at all limited to worship of the God of Israel in the Jerusalem temple. Religious rituals took place not only in the Jerusalem temple, for which there is unfortunately no archaeological evidence, but also among the clans scattered throughout the countryside, where fertility rituals and other pagan practices were widespread. In fact, a late-monarchic inscription from Judah indicates that pagan cults were rife not only in rural districts but in Jerusalem. It is now clear that the God of Israel was worshiped in Jerusalem along with many other deities, especially Baal, Asherah, the hosts of heaven, and even the national gods of other states.

Emergence of Monotheism

When the Assyrians left the northern kingdom in the late eighth century, the archaeological evidence indicates that Judah experienced sudden population growth and social evolution and thus finally achieved statehood. Along with this social transformation there arose intense religious struggle. Before this time, as we've seen, religious ideas and practices were quite diverse and dispersed in both northern and southern kingdoms. But after the departure of the Assyrians, there was increasing centralization in Judah, and within a short time in the late eighth and early seventh centuries BCE, a tradition of monotheism emerged. This newly emerged tradition considered the cults in the countryside to be sinful, and the God of Israel became the only acceptable object of worship.

With this social revolution came the expansion of bureaucratic administration and of literacy. This period was then perfect for the creation of literature, and the God-of-Israel-Alone movement used literature to promote its ideology, especially in the book of Deuteronomy and in the Deuteronomistic History, which includes Deuteronomy through 2 Kings. Exactly when this God-of-Israel-Alone theology became a determining factor in the affairs of state in Judah is uncertain, but the Deuteronomistic History highlights the reign of Hezekiah as such a moment (2 Kgs 18:3–7). It is then that Judah appears as the center of the people of Israel, and Jerusalem becomes the center of the worship of the God of Israel.

In an attempt to free Judah from Assyria, which was the region's cruel landlord, Hezekiah revolted against Assyria. The Deuteronomistic History claimed that God would intervene to save Judah (2 Kgs 19:6–7, 32–34), but the reality is that the Assyrian king, Sennacherib, devastated the Judahite countryside, especially the agriculturally rich Shephalah foothills, and thus destroyed the economic base of the rebellious kingdom. Archaeological surveys show that the region never recovered from Sennacherib's campaign. Only Jerusalem and the area directly south of the city were spared. Thus, despite the Deuteronomistic History's tale of

Hezekiah's piety and God's intervention, Judah was actually reduced to poverty and subjugated to Assyria.

When Hezekiah died in 689 BCE, his twelve-year-old son, Manasseh, became king. His first priority was the economic reconstruction of Judah. But this could be accomplished only through cooperation with the rural networks of village elders and clans, and that meant returning to polytheism. For this reason the Deuteronomistic History describes Manasseh as the most sinful monarch Judah had ever known (2 Kgs 21:3–7). In any case, under Manasseh, Judah became integrated into the Assyrian economy, particularly by trading in exotic luxury goods, incense from Arabia, and olive oil.

The kings Ahaz, Hezekiah, and Manasseh all had the dream of uniting the entire Israelite population: one capital, one temple, and one dynasty. But Assyria was still too strong for that dream to be realized. All Judah could do was submit to Assyria and wait for the right moment to break away. Ahaz made Judah prosperous although in exchange for permitting traditional pagan practices. Hezekiah launched a religious reform, but it resulted in disaster. Manasseh restored the economy, but at the expense of even more polytheism.

Josiah's Reform

Manasseh died in 642 BCE and was replaced by his son Amon, who only two years later was assassinated. Amon's eight-year-old son, Josiah, was then placed on the throne. In 622 BCE, Josiah, as if playing a messianic role, launched the most intense puritan reform in the history of Judah. According to the Deuteronomistic historian, Josiah rid the temple of idolatrous rites (2 Kgs 23:4–7), eradicated the shrines of foreign cults (2 Kgs 23:10–14), put an end to the sacrificial rituals performed by rural priests at scattered high places and shrines in the countryside (2 Kgs 23:15–18), purged the shrines in the former northern kingdom (2 Kgs 23:19–20), and instituted celebration of the Passover. The crucial moment in this reform was the public reading of the book of the Law, widely believed to be the book of Deuteronomy, which was written just before Josiah's reform.

Observing this law would constitute the people's repentance for centuries of sin. Deuteronomy prohibits worship anywhere but in the temple of Jerusalem and spells out the basic principles of this reform movement. It also promulgates ethical laws and social welfare provisions that have no parallel in any other texts in the Hebrew Bible. All these changes in Judah were possible only because of the decline in Assyrian power and influence. Because of this decline, Judah at last enjoyed a measure of independence.

Unfortunately, the archaeological evidence for Josiah's reform is weak. For example, the temple of Bethel has not yet been found. Meanwhile the seals and impressions of late-monarchic Judahite officials, though different from those of earlier periods in Judah, are similar to those in Ammon and Moab, so that this change in styles may simply be the result of spreading literacy and thus not be any indication of a reform. Other evidence indicates that Josiah was unable to stop the veneration of idols. For example, small figurines of Asherah have been found in abundance in private homes dating from the time of Josiah.

As Assyrian power waned, Egypt experienced a renewal and set out to fulfill its centuries-long dream of dominating all of Canaan. In 610 BCE the pharaoh Necho II led a military expedition northward to assist the enfeebled Assyrian empire in its fight against the Babylonians. Josiah apparently saw this Egyptian military action as a threat to Judah's independence because, at the head of what could only have been a relatively puny army, he went out to do battle with Necho II and was killed. Assyrian power continued to decline while Babylonian power soared.

Exile, Return, and Rebuilding

After the death of Josiah, his reform movement collapsed, and the Deuteronomistic History describes the last two decades of Judah's history as a period of unrelenting decline. For a while Egypt tried to maintain control of Canaan, but in 605 BCE the Babylonian crown prince later known as Nebuchadnezzar defeated the Egyptian army at Carchemish (Jer 46:2). Then he put severe pressure on Jerusalem (2 Kgs 24:10–16), laid siege to the city, and deported the Jerusalem priesthood and aristocracy to exile in Babylon. Zedekiah, the last king in the Davidic dynasty, was blinded and imprisoned in Babylon, and his sons were slaughtered. The temple of Jerusalem was destroyed. Every late-monarchic site excavated in Judah shows evidence of the Babylonian invasion and of the continuous decline of the southern kingdom.

Little is known about the life of the exiles in Babylon, except that they had a long stay: fifty years. But their exile ended abruptly when the Persians defeated the Neo-Babylonian empire in 539 BCE, and Cyrus, founder of the Persian empire, issued a decree authorizing the restoration of Judah and the temple (Ezra 1:2–3). A leader among the exiles named Sheshbazzar led a group of about fifty thousand people back to Jerusalem and laid the foundations for a new temple. A few years later, Jeshua led another group of returnees back to Jerusalem where they built an altar and celebrated the Feast of Tabernacles (Ezra 3:11–13). The people of Samaria, that is, the deportees who had been brought there by the Assyrians, heard about this construction work and offered to help, but Jeshua and Zerubbabel rejected their offer because, so the returnees believed, only they were divinely entitled to build the new temple and to determine who could be a member of Judahite orthodoxy.

The new temple was completed in 516 BCE, but nothing remarkable happened until Ezra, a scribe skilled in the law of Moses, arrived in Jerusalem from Babylon in 458 BCE with money and judicial authority from Artaxerxes, king of Persia. Ezra was shocked by the fact that the returnees were marrying polytheists and still following the pagan practices of their neighbors. He then banished foreign wives.

Nehemiah, a high court official of the Persian king, arrived in Jerusalem in 445 BCE and summoned the returnees to join in solidarity to rebuild the walls of the city. Despite being hindered by Judah's neighbors, he succeeded in rebuilding the walls. He also implemented social legislation that restored land to the poor and prohibited the charging of interest. Like Ezra, he prohibited intermarriage.

Theological Problems and Community Building

In spite of God's unconditional promise to David regarding the eternal rule of the Davidic dynasty in Jerusalem—this promise being the basis of the Deuteronomistic faith—the Judahites in exile had lost everything that was dear to them: their homes, their land, their temple, their independence. In fact, their identity itself was in question. The way to reassert their identity was for them to edit the Deuteronomistic History—not only in order to fill in the history from Josiah to the exile—but to reconcile God's unconditional promise with all their losses. The most conspicuous changes to the Deuteronomistic History involved making God's promise conditional on Israel's walking before God (1 Kgs 8:25) and also putting blame for the disaster entirely on Manasseh, who was portrayed as the wickedest of all Judahite kings. Moreover, Josiah's righteousness was pictured as only slowing the ineluctable destruction of Jerusalem (2 Kgs 22:18–20). The net change was that the rewritten Deuteronomistic History subordinated God's covenant with David to God's covenant with the people of Israel at Sinai.

Archaeologists estimate the population of Judah before the deportations as about seventy-five thousand, there being about fifteen thousand in Jerusalem. The highest possible figure for the number of exiles is thought to be twenty thousand. Hence at least 75 percent of Judah's population remained on the land and continued to pursue their agricultural activity. Contrary to traditional scholarly opinion, life continued uninterrupted in the area both north and south of Jerusalem from the destruction of Jerusalem in 586 BCE until the proclamation of Cyrus in 538 BCE. Data from surveys of all the settlements in the postexilic community of the time of Ezra and Nehemiah (henceforth this community is referred to by its name as a Persian province: Yehud) indicate that the population of Yehud was only thirty thousand. The returnees were a minority in Yehud, but their prestige as survivors of the exile, along with their religious, socioeconomic, and political status, gave them considerable power, especially since they were concentrated in Jerusalem. Thus the returnees were able to establish their authority over the population of Yehud.

Once the temple was rebuilt, in 516 BCE, the Davidic family no longer played a role in the history of Yehud. Instead the Yehud community adopted a dual system of governance: for politics, Persian-appointed governors with no links to the Davidic line and, for religious matters, priests. Without kingship, the temple became the identity-defining center of Yehud life.

The priests were responsible for the continuing production of literature, the purpose of which was to build group identity, especially in terms of the Yehud community's norms vis-à-vis its neighbors. The rise of the priesthood in the postexilic community harmonizes both with the idea that the final editing of the Pentateuch was done in this period and with the appearance of the Priestly source (P), the author responsible for Gen 1:1—2:4a. It should be noted that the needs of the postexilic state were similar to those of Judah in the late-monarchic period. That is, the Yehud community had hostile neighbors; it claimed territory outside its realm; and it had to confront problems of purity and assimilation. Thus most of the texts produced during the reign of Josiah were very helpful to the Yehud community as well. But because the Davidic house was now out of the picture, the Yehud community had to do some reworking of ideas. For example, the Yehud community reshaped the Exodus narrative so that there would be an exact parallel between the bondage in Egypt and the bondage in Babylon, as well as between the two experiences of exodus. In this way the postexilic editing of the Hebrew Bible was designed to recapitulate ideas useful to the Yehud community while making the Hebrew Bible itself, rather than Davidic kingship, the central authority of the community.

Now I will close the chapter with a few of my own observations.

My Comments

Given the fact that Finkelstein and Silberman analyze and interpret mega-amounts of archaeological data, it is unreasonable to expect that there would be a scholarly consensus on their results. Undoubtedly, scholars will continue to find fault here and there, either with the data itself or with Finkelstein and Silberman's interpretation of them. But it is important to remember that no matter how many holes scholars are able to punch in what Finkelstein and Silberman say about the patriarchs, the exodus, or the wilderness wandering, the general conclusions of these two authors still hold true. How so? It's because the key element in their argument is the alleged invasion and conquest of Canaan by the Israelites. If the Israelites did not invade and conquer Canaan, then there was no wilderness wandering and, consequently, no exodus either, and, as a result, the biblical account of Israel's history summarily loses whatever credibility it had as historical. Importantly, all the archaeological evidence indicates that the Israelites had been residents of Canaan well before it experienced major social and political changes around 1200 BCE, and there is no evidence at all to support the theory that the Israelites were responsible for producing those changes—and certainly not by force of arms. In fact, the archaeological evidence is that Israelite settlements in Canaan at that time did not even have weapons.

What all this means is that there is little choice but to accept Finkelstein and Silberman's interpretation of the archaeological evidence as more or less correct and reliable and agree with them that the real history of Israel is vastly different from the Hebrew Bible's accounts of it. One also must agree with Finkelstein and Silberman in affirming that many texts in the Hebrew Bible are much later, that is, more recent, than previously thought. Otherwise, we would have to believe that great literary texts emerged in Israel before the Israelites had even achieved literacy. The most useful step to take at this point may be to turn our attention to the question of literary production. But, first, let us comment on the significance of the fact that the narratives concerning the patriarchs, the exodus, the wilderness wandering, and the conquest are not based upon actual historical events.

At first one might think that the nearly complete lack of historical basis for these narratives would invalidate them, and of course it does invalidate them as factual reporting. But their very lack of historical validity makes them all the greater as literature. The brilliant accomplishment of the authors of Genesis through 2 Kings was to invent exactly the pseudo-historical propaganda that was necessary in order for Josiah and, later, the Yehud community to propagate the monotheism that had started to emerge in Israel under Hezekiah and Josiah. These narratives were much more effective in achieving their intended purpose than any merely factual account of Israel's real history would have been. These biblical authors deserve immense credit for shaping and expressing that emerging monotheism, which, for all practical purposes, they created. Thus, they were not reliable historians, but they were religious and literary geniuses. So, then, on to the question of literary production.

Finkelstein and Silberman argue that the reign of Josiah, when literacy finally became widespread in Judah, was a period of enormous literary production. In their view, not only the book of Deuteronomy and the Deuteronomistic History (which was the first ever continuous history of Israel) but also the patriarchal narratives, the exodus and wilderness wandering narrative, and the conquest narratives were all written during the reign of Josiah, essentially as propaganda for his reform. Finkelstein and Silberman show convincingly how this literature served the purposes of that reform. They therefore affirm that Josiah's reform should be thought of as the crowning moment of Israel's history.

Before we present the trophy to Josiah, however, let's consider some other factors: (1) Josiah's reform lasted a mere twelve years, and, according to Finkelstein and Silberman, although it had its victories, its results were more theoretical than practical; in practice the reform failed to eliminate polytheism in Judah; (2) although Josiah's reign may be responsible for the production of the patriarchal narratives, the exodus narrative, and the conquest narratives, these still existed only as independent, unconnected stories and thus did not have the meaning they came to have in their final form, which was given to them by the Yehud community; as we will explain more fully in our next chapter, Genesis through 2 Kings have an underlying metaphorical structure that depends upon creation theology, which did not emerge in Israel until after the Babylonian exile; (3) although Josiah's reform contained most of the central features of biblical monotheism, its main theological premise—God's unconditional promise to the Davidic line—was a serious mistake that the Yehud community had to correct; and (4) the most important part of the Hebrew Bible is the Torah (Pentateuch), which is a product of the Yehud community. Thus, it seems that Josiah's reform did indeed start something wonderful but left it flawed and unfinished for the Yehud community to correct, amplify, and perfect.

Clearly, the very existence of the Yehud community represents a monumental reform, and we're talking about a reform that endured and had great success. By comparison, Josiah's reform looks like a quixotic fantasy. In fact, the aftermath of Josiah's reform shows just how fragile a fantasy it was. Moreover, though the literary accomplishments of Josiah's reign are undeniably great, those of the Yehud community appear even greater, a point we will expand upon in the following chapter.

4

More about Structure

THE HEBREW BIBLE IS famously divided into three sections: Torah (Pentateuch), Neviim (Prophets), and Kethuvim (Writings). But these are only divisions of convenience. The Hebrew Bible's real structure lies much deeper and has to do with the destruction/re-creation paradigm we discussed in chapter 2. There we saw that every important stage in Israel's history is marked by a destruction/re-creation, which serves as the framework upon which the (real or imaginary) events of Israel's history are hung. We should note that not every destruction/re-creation carried out by God was necessarily effective. The great flood, as we've seen, was only partially successful, and the exodus started out looking like a huge success but proved to be a failure because the Israelites once freed from bondage refused to do what God had freed them to do—namely, love and obey God.

Something similar can be said for Josiah's reform, which was a destruction/re-creation that looked brilliant for a moment and then fizzled out. What's absolutely remarkable about the exile/Yehud community is that it represents both a very radical destruction—literally everything the exiled Israelites once had was gone—and an equally radical re-creation in which the central features of biblical monotheism were no longer mere theoretical ideals but a living reality on a community-wide basis. In other words, through the exile and the Yehud community, God at long last achieved a satisfying

More about Structure

and enduring victory in God's long struggle to produce an exemplary community of faithful agents and conversation partners.

In light of what we have learned about the literary production and lasting power of the Yehud community, as compared with Josiah's reform, we can conclude that the metaphorical structure of Israel's history in Genesis through 2 Kings—that is, creation followed by repeated destruction/re-creation—reaches its logical climax not in Josiah's reform but in the exile and the Yehud community. That fact tells us that the Hebrew Bible was edited from the Babylonian exile backward, which is to say that the exclusive loyalty to the God of Israel and the group cohesion found in the Yehud community are the goal toward which all that precedes aims. The emergence of the Yehud community is the organizing principle and reason for being of Genesis through 2 Kings. God's long pursuit of the goal of producing a genuinely faithful and enduring community consistently takes the form of a destruction-re-creation cycle, which is a structure that depends, as pointed out several times, on creation theology, which appears in Israel only after the exile. That's what we mean when we say that the Yehud community is the starting point for a retrospective that will make the emergence of that community seem like the fulfillment of God's promises and plans. Everything that comes before the amazing destruction/re-creation that is the exile/Yehud community is prelude to it and is designed to make it understandable.

It is fair to say, then, that the Yehud community represents the best of God's destruction–re-creation cycles because it really worked and lasted. In terms of God's plan to mold Israel into an obedient community that would remain faithful over time, the Yehud community is clearly the highpoint of the whole story and far outshines anything in the time of Josiah. By the way, if the Deuteronomistic History in its final form dismisses kingship and elevates the temple as the center of community solidarity, it does so not only because it was convenient to blame the kings for the long centuries of Israelite polytheism but because kingship, for all its alleged glories, historically proved incapable of generating the level of community cohesion and solidarity that popular participation in the temple could generate and that the Yehud community needed if it was to endure.

The main theological difficulty that arose for the Yehud community is that, on the one hand, it replaced kingship with the temple and condemned virtually everything and everyone in the monarchical period, but on the other hand it claimed somehow to be a revival and therefore not a new religion. But if preexilic Israel was so idolatrous, how could a revival of something from that period qualify as exclusive loyalty to the God of Israel? The solution that the Yehud community found, in addition to reediting the Deuteronomistic History, was to commission the writing of a second, alternative history of Israel, and this is found in 1 and 2 Chronicles. The Chronicles present a radically revised picture of Israel's history in which the temple is the center of attention. What's special and new about its treatment of the temple is the author's repeated emphasis on the popular nature of the temple. In Chronicles the preexilic temple is described—and this is of course pure propaganda—as if it had been a community center in which all Israelites regularly participated. But in fact there is no evidence at all that the preexilic temple had such a character. Far from being popular, the temple was a royal institution. Therefore we should understand that this characterization of the preexilic temple in Chronicles as a popular institution is propaganda designed to help make the temple into a popular institution in the Yehud community. We can infer that it was very important in the Yehud community for the temple to become a genuinely popular institution.

Chronicles also emphasize the importance of the Davidic dynasty—not in the sense that the Yehud community actually wanted a king—but for the purpose of pretending that the monarchy (the house of David) existed mainly for the sake of the temple. In this way the fundamentally idolatrous character of most of Israel's monarchs is pushed into the background, and they appear somehow cloaked in glory as representatives of the Davidic line and thus, importantly, defenders of the temple.

A third emphasis in Chronicles is on the question of how those who lived in what was once the northern kingdom or those who had not participated in the exile experience could receive God's mercy and blessing. This emphasis shows that the Yehud community was trying hard to build a constituency among those many people who had Israelite ethnicity but had not had the exile experience, including those living in the Diaspora.

If, however, this postexilic loyalty to the God of Israel were not something radically new, if it were simply the revival of something already accepted and familiar, none of these mighty propagandistic efforts would be necessary. Hence the reality is that this exclusive loyalty to the God of Israel in the Yehud community should be seen as radically new. Those who experienced the exile are attempting to make their newfound loyalty to the God of Israel normative for all people of Israelite ethnicity.

To get an idea of how far this religion in fact was from being normative, at least initially, we need to take into account that the vast majority of all ethnic Israelites in the northern territories or the southern kingdom did not have the experience of exile. For them exclusive loyalty to the God of Israel was a new and bizarre notion contrary to their time-honored polytheistic traditions. Moreover, though the books of Ezra and Nehemiah focus on the situation in Jerusalem where the returnees were clustered, most people of Israelite ethnicity lived outside Jerusalem, including in the Diaspora, that is, in countries other than Israel. Let us therefore now consider the case of one of the most important Diaspora communities: Elephantina. For this discussion we are indebted to the pioneering research of historian Simon Schama, *A História dos Judeus: Encontrar as palavras 1000 A.C.–1492 D.C.*, vol. 1.

Schama's View of a Particular Community in the Diaspora

Elephantina was a southern Egyptian town established by Egypt's then-rulers, the Persians, in the last third of the sixth century BCE for the purpose of defending Egypt's southern border. This border outpost had a large Israelite population made up of people who had fled to Egypt either from the northern kingdom at the time of the Assyrian invasion toward the end of the eighth century BCE or from Judah at the time of the Babylonian invasion at the beginning of the sixth century BCE. Most of these Israelites were employed as professional soldiers. As in so many Israelite communities situated in a Gentile environment, the religion practiced by Israelites in Elephantina was worldly, cosmopolitan, and vernacular. Israelites there spoke Aramaic, not Hebrew, and tended to have mundane interests such as property, fashion, money, marriages, divorces, and children. They were fully involved in all the local Gentile social activities and at the same time followed some sort of Israelite ritual calendar. Importantly, the Torah was not found in the Elephantine archive. Clearly, in Schama's view, this community was formed before the Torah became inflexible and widely distributed. The Elephantine community also had their own monumental temple (the very existence of which, we should note, contradicted Deuteronomistic theology).

In many ways the city of Elephantina was quite different from Jerusalem, especially because in Jerusalem the community of returnees from the exile lived a segregated existence. Elephantina, however, had no closed neighborhood for Israelites. Instead people of the most diverse backgrounds lived as neighbors, and marriage contracts found in Elephantina indicate that Israelites frequently married Gentiles. Quite unlike the history of Jerusalem, the history of the Elephantine community was, in Schama's words, a history "without martyrs, wisemen, or philosophical quarrels."[1] This was a place of "happy banalities, given to real estate disputes, elegant clothes, weddings, and parties, where tough young soldiers lived next door to even tougher Gentile boatmen; a place of ointments and cozy hideaways, where people skipped stones on the river and rested in the shade of palm trees, at a time and in a place completely removed from the romanticism of suffering."[2]

Interestingly, the Israelites living in Elephantina celebrated Passover but in a completely different way from the Yehud community. In Elephantina they celebrated their liberation from the

1. Schama, *História dos Judeus*, 49, my translation.
2. Ibid., my translation.

Assyrians and the Babylonians and thanked God for bringing them to Egypt.

My Comments

It may be that Elephantina is not entirely typical of what the Diaspora was like during the time of Ezra and Nehemiah, but it seems safe to assume that, like Elephantina, Diaspora communities had a number of practices that deviated significantly from the norm that the Yehud community in Jerusalem was trying to impose. We should remember that Ezra was commissioned by the Persian king Artaxerxes to correct the deviant practices of those who had remained behind in Jerusalem after the Babylonian pillage of the city and who were suspected by the exiles of leading impure lives, adopting pagan customs, and marrying foreign women (Ezra 7:25–26). In other words, the Yehud community was well aware of such deviant practices.

It should therefore not surprise us that, in 419 BCE, Ananias, a close relative of Nehemiah, wrote a letter to the Israelite community in Elephantina in order to correct their deviant practices. In fact, Ananias later appeared in person in Elephantina and gave the Israelites living there very strict instructions regarding the Passover.[3] Since the obvious purpose of Ananias' mission was to impose conformity on the Elephantina community, we should conclude that the Yehud community in Jerusalem was experiencing anxiety about the deviationist practices of Israelites living in Egypt and in the Diaspora generally.

The example of Elephantina seems quite sufficient to prove our point that the Yehud community in Jerusalem, with its emphasis on strict Torah observance and on separation from Gentiles, was indeed practicing a new religion and creating a new model for Israelite life. The normative religion they were imposing was decidedly not the revival of something old and established. The community of returnees from exile in Jerusalem was expecting

3. Ibid., 40.

other people of Israelite ethnicity living outside Jerusalem or in the Diaspora to conform to norms that were actually quite strange for people who had not had the experience of exile.

At least in terms of the literature of the Hebrew Bible, we can see that the Yehud community in Jerusalem was quite successful in having its way. Everything from Deuteronomy through 2 Kings, plus 1 and 2 Chronicles and the books of Ezra and Nehemiah, reinforces the theology of this puritan movement, which is the theology of retribution. The book of Joshua may very well have been written, as we have seen Finkelstein and Silberman suggest, to express Josiah's fantasies of territorial expansion, but the Yehud community would also have found that book to be very useful because it makes inheritance of the land depend on Israel's keeping the Torah, and thus the book of Joshua reinforces the theology of retribution. If Israel sins, it must be punished, and it is restored only when it repents. In fact, the theology of all the various books just mentioned is the theology of retribution, according to which God rewards obedience to the torah and punishes disobedience. The immense impact that the Yehud community had upon the people of Israel can be measured by the pervasive presence of that theology not only in Genesis through 2 Kings but in the Prophets, in the Psalms, and in Proverbs.

If, however, we consider certain other books in the Hebrew Bible, we can see that the Yehud (and later simply the Jewish) community in Jerusalem never fully succeeded in imposing its will on all people of Israelite ethnicity. For example, the (late postexilic) book of Ecclesiastes mocks the notion that God rewards virtue and punishes evil, and the (late postexilic) book of Job refutes entirely the idea that God is bound by any such principle. The (late postexilic) book of Jonah is even stronger in its rejection of the theology of retribution by portraying God as so unconfined by that theology and so eager to forgive those who repent that God will forgive even those mega-sinners, the Ninevites—without even punishing them.

On the question of separation from Gentiles, we have the (late postexilic) book of Ruth, in which a Moabite woman (the Moabites being one of Israel's oldest and most despised enemies)

More about Structure

proves remarkably faithful to her Israelite mother-in-law and to God's instructions. By the hidden action of God, Ruth becomes the great-grandmother of King David. We also have the marvelous story of the Gentile prostitute Rahab in Joshua 2. She has amazing courage and confidence in God, but, more than that, she shows a far deeper understanding of God's intentions than do the Israelite spies she saves and protects. The existence of such stories in the Hebrew Bible, especially the book of Ruth, is more than enough to indicate that some postexilic Israelites thought not only that it was unwise to separate from Gentiles but that at least some Gentiles might understand more about God than did Israelites. That was a very daring affirmation for this literature to make and was clearly a rebuke of the Yehud movement.

Overall, the agenda of the Yehud movement is dominant in the Hebrew Bible. It features, in particular, the theology of retribution, strict observance of the torah, separation from Gentiles, popular participation in the temple, and belief in the eternal character of the Davidic dynasty, though this latter belief did not imply that the Yehud movement wanted to be ruled by a king. Its opinions about the monarchy, as we have seen, are somewhat contradictory.

It's important to bear in mind, however, that the Yehud movement and its ideas, though predominant in the Hebrew Bible and in postexilic Israel, by no means enjoyed consensus support either in the Hebrew Bible itself or among all Israelites, whether in Israel or in the Diaspora. For that reason we should not be surprised to discover that in later Jewish literature, like the New Testament, this movement's ideas get challenged.

5

Messianic Expectation

THE EARLY CHURCH, TO advance its own proclamation of Jesus as the messiah, made certain changes to the Hebrew Bible (or actually to the Greek translation of it, the LXX). The most notable change was rearranging the order of texts, so that the Christian collection (the Old Testament) ends with the book of Malachi. In the Jewish order of texts the collection ends with 2 Chronicles. Q: What difference does that make? A: A lot. The last verse in the book of Malachi reads, "Lo, I will send the prophet Elijah to you before the coming of the awesome, fearful day of the Lord." By making the Old Testament end with Malachi, the early church tried to make it seem as if the Jews were eagerly anticipating the awesome, fearful day of the Lord: the messiah's appearance. But that was not necessarily true. Jews would surely have liked for the messiah to come; his coming would be welcome at any time. But among Jews the coming of the messiah was (and still is) much more something to be piously hoped for than imminently expected. Only three times in the three millennia–long history of the Jews did they become excited about the possible coming of the messiah, and all three such moments of heightened expectation proved disappointing or even disastrous. The rest of the time the Jews curbed their enthusiasm. How could their expectation of the messiah remain so lacking in urgency?

It's because the Yehud community came into existence as a result of the Israelites' repentance during the exile. The exile/Yehud community serves as strong evidence that God is willing to forgive the people of Israel whenever they sincerely repent. Therefore Jews believe strongly in the power of repentance. They hope and believe that if they repent, God will perform a destruction/re-creation that liberates them from whatever mess they may be in and re-creates them. Such, after all, is the paradigm governing all of Israel's experience with God, and it's the theme of Rosh Hashanah, Yom Kippur, and especially Pesach (Passover). The messiah, on the other hand, should he ever come, will be expected to do much more than liberate and re-create. For example, he will gather to Jerusalem all the Jews who over the centuries have been dispersed, will put an end to war and effect a genuine peace, will cause all the nations to bow down before the God of Israel, and will make them recognize Israel as God's chosen people. The Jews would of course like for all these things to happen, but they're not holding their breath.

The Hebrew Bible, by contrast with the Old testament, ends with 2 Chronicles, whose concluding verse reads, "Thus said King Cyrus of Persia: The Lord God has given me all the kingdoms of the earth, and has charged me with building Him a House in Jerusalem, which is in Judah. Any one of you of all His people, the Lord his God be with him and let him go up" (2 Chr 36:23 JPS Hebrew-English Tanakh). What does it mean to conclude the Hebrew Bible in this way?

It means that the Jew is pictured as living—not in expectation of the imminent arrival of the messiah—but in gratitude to God for the destruction/re-creation God has performed that liberates him from bondage so that he can embark on a pilgrimage to Jerusalem. Thus the Jew is pictured as a happy pilgrim. His gratitude to God translates quite naturally to a life not only of repentance but of joyful commitment to doing *mitzvoth* (literally, "commandments," but understood as good works). Thus the Jew is seen at the end of 2 Chronicles as embracing a life of faithful observance of the torah and joy-filled pilgrimage. This ending to the Hebrew Bible suggests no preoccupation at all with the coming of the messiah.

Thus, messianic expectation, though certainly not unknown among Jews, is far more intense among Christians. In any case, it is a mistake for Christians to criticize Jews for not accepting Jesus as their messiah. The fact is that Jesus did not fulfill any of the expectations that Jews had for the messiah. He therefore cannot possibly be considered the messiah of the Jews. On the other hand, if Christians want to claim Jesus as *their* messiah, that's something different.

6

Socio-religious Origins of Jesus of Nazareth

WE HAVE ALREADY SEEN that the Yehud movement became normative in Jerusalem but was not able to convince all people of Israelite ethnicity; that pockets of resistance remained in Israel and in the Diaspora; that the Hebrew Bible has excellent texts designed to refute the claims of the Yehud movement; and that Jews living in the Diaspora were likely to disagree with those claims. Significantly, one of the defining facts about Jesus of Nazareth may be that he was from Nazareth in the Galilee. Scholars have long recognized that the Galilee was a place rather remote culturally and geographically from Jerusalem, that it was a melting pot of nationalities and languages, and that Jews there lived in close proximity to Gentiles. So different was the Galilee from Jerusalem that, for all practical purposes, the Galilee was part of the Diaspora. In short, it was just the sort of place where Jews could be expected to hold liberal views opposed to those of the religious establishment in Jerusalem.

Take, for example, the question of Jewish separation from Gentiles or from other sources of impurity. In the Gospel of Mark, we see Jesus in close contact with demons, lepers, demon-possessed people, and even dead bodies, and he categorically rejects the Levitical distinction between clean and unclean (Mark 7:1–23). Throughout this gospel he also has frequent contact with women. He even gets instructed by a Syro-Phoenician woman

55

(Mark 7:24–30), and Syro-Phoenicia, we should recall, was known to Jews as the traditional source of the worst idolatry ever introduced into Israel. This Syro-Phoenician woman is a parade example of a Gentile who understands God better than most Jews—and even better than Jesus. In all these ways, Jesus is a voice of protest against the xenophobia and sexism of the Yehud movement.

On the question of the Sabbath, Jesus teaches (Mark 2:23—3:6) that compassion, which was of course important not only to Jesus but to all Jews, takes precedence even over Sabbath observance, and that the Torah, properly understood, is intended more to inspire compassion than to demand strict observance. Here again Jesus voices opposition to the Judaism that had become normative. Curiously, the Talmud is closer to Jesus on this point than were some of Jesus' contemporaries, because it permits the rescuing of animals on the Sabbath if they're in danger.[1]

As for the theology of retribution, Jesus rejects it in every conceivable way. Instead of wanting to punish the sinner, Jesus acts much more like God in the book of Jonah. In fact, Jesus is so eager to forgive that he tells the story of a father who forgives his sinful son even before the young man has had a chance to ask for forgiveness (Luke 15:11–31).

On the Yehud insistence that the Jerusalem temple is the only legitimate place to worship the God of Israel, Jesus declares that the temple has been thoroughly corrupted and has therefore lost all legitimacy (Mark 11:12–19). We should recall that the Yehud movement had chosen the temple to be the touchstone of Jewish identity. The implication, then, is that the movement itself is thoroughly corrupt. Jesus also thinks that the temple ought to be a house of prayer for all nations (Mark 11:17). The generous inclusivity of this last statement is in stark contrast to the call for separation from Gentiles.

Jesus was obviously opposed to the Judaism that had become normative earlier under Ezra and Nehemiah and that continued as normative in the period of Jesus. What's interesting about his opposition, from both literary and socio-political viewpoints, is

---

1. Ibid., 236.

that Jesus appears to be a spiritual descendant of the books of Job, Jonah and Ruth, all of which oppose normative Judaism in general and its xenophobia and theology of retribution in particular. A clear continuity runs between those texts and the ideas of Jesus. Certainly, then, Jesus is not innovating so much as he is voicing opposition that had been around for a long time. His opposition is in fact thoroughly Jewish, with deep historical roots and strong connections to Jews living in Diaspora-like environments. Even Jesus' famous insistence on loving your enemy is Jewish, but for Jerusalem Jews, who lived segregated from foreigners, love of one's enemies was not a priority. Jerusalem Jews might collaborate with the Romans, profit from them, and tolerate their presence, but that certainly didn't stop them from hating their Roman occupiers. In any case, normative Judaism does not appear to have a mechanism or procedure for dealing with non-Jewish enemies. The situation for Galilean or Diaspora Jews, however, would have been quite different. Galilean or Diaspora Jews, who lived in racially and religiously mixed neighborhoods, who might have a foreign wife or husband and foreign relatives, and who might live right next door to Romans or other foreign enemies, would be much more likely to value the importance of being reconciled with one's enemies and therefore to seek a mechanism or procedure for achieving such reconciliation. By the way, the fact that Jesus preached reconciliation with enemies also indicates how faithful Jesus was to the Torah, because thirty-six times, far more than any other commandment, the Torah emphasizes loving the other, the person who is different from you.

7

Jewish Ethics and the Ethics of Jesus of Nazareth

IT MAY SEEM STRANGE to bring up the subject of ethics in a reflection on the Hebrew Bible as literature, but the Hebrew Bible's own emphasis on ethics makes a discussion of it relevant. As we saw in chapter 1, the first text in the Hebrew Bible proclaims that we humans are made in the image and after the likeness of God and that we are to act as God's agents, doing what God would do on earth if God were here. In short, we humans are all supposed to imitate God, so that ethics properly understood is imitation of God.

We saw in Gen 2–11 that, except for Noah, humans failed badly in their assigned task and therefore that God chose one particular people whose responsibility it would be to model this imitation of God. To help them do so, God eventually provides them with the torah, a set of instructions that, no matter how complicated these may be in places, are all designed to facilitate imitation of God. In fact, God not only institutes the precepts of the torah but sets an example by fulfilling them himself/herself. That is, God doesn't ask Israel to do anything that God does not already do. Hence the instruction in Deut 13:5 to follow—that is, imitate—God. So what is this example that God sets? The following discussion of the basics of Jewish ethics is indebted to Abraham Cohen.[1]

---

1. Ibid., 210–37.

In Gen 3:21, Adam and Eve face a difficult future and need clothes, and so God makes clothes for them. Hence our responsibility to clothe the naked. In Gen 18:1–14, God visits Abraham and Sarah in their old age. Hence our responsibility to visit the sick and aged. In this same passage Abraham welcomes three strangers. Hence our responsibility to be hospitable to travelers and wayfarers. In Gen 25:11, God comforts Isaac upon the death of Abraham and Sarah. Hence our responsibility to comfort those who mourn.

As Deut 11:22 puts it, the Israelites are commanded to walk in God's ways and hold fast to God. Deuteronomy 34:6 explains what these ways are: "a God compassionate and gracious, slow to anger, abounding in kindness and faithfulness." God is good to all, supports all who stumble and gives open-handedly (Ps 145). Hence we are to do likewise. Of course, God can also be angry, but anger is a divine prerogative forbidden to humans. Leviticus 19:18 cautions us against taking vengeance or bearing a grudge and commands us instead to love our neighbor as ourselves. So, then, let us begin with the first area of ethical concern: brotherly love.

Talmudic Ethics

Brotherly Love

We are commanded to love our neighbor as ourselves, but who is our neighbor? "Neighbor" is understood especially as the one who is different from us. Exodus 23:4 demonstrates this point: "When you encounter your enemy's ox or ass wandering, you must take it back to him." Here neighbor includes not only the stranger but the idolater, whose religion is inimical to one's own. Hence our responsibility toward other humans must take precedence over our personal dislikes and antagonisms and must apply even to those who actively oppose us. It should also be noted that taking good care of your enemy's property could do much to turn an enemy into a friend.

We are commanded not only to love but also not to hate. Leviticus 19:17 reads: "You shall not hate your kinsfolk in your heart." This example helps also to show that what God desires from us is not simply the right behavior but the right behavior springing from the right motivation.

Thus the first component in Jewish ethics is brotherly love carried out with loving motivation. This is obviously a wonderful, God-like behavior, but humility may be even better. Moses, who more than anyone else in the Hebrew Bible had reason to boast, is described as exceptionally humble (Exod 12:3). Moreover, it is to the humble that the prophet, full of the spirit of God, announces the good news (Isa 61:1), but "every haughty person is an abomination to the Lord" (Prov 16:5).

Charity

Just as God helps and protects Adam and Eve, rescues the Israelites from Egypt, feeds them in the wilderness, and gives them a promised land, so we are expected to be as helpful as possible to those in need. This kind of helpfulness can be thought of as both charity and justice. If we recall that the Israelites are not properly owners of the promised land but only tenants, God being the real owner, then whatever they have is really on loan from God. By giving to charity, they help to achieve a more equitable distribution of what God has loaned. Thus, helping the poor is both an act of charity and an act of justice. Charity/justice is perhaps the closest we humans can come to imitating the divine loving-kindness.

Deuteronomy 15:8 adds something important on this subject. It reads: "You must open your hand and lend him [your kinsman] sufficient for whatever he needs." The idea here is that, instead of making someone dependent on your welfare, your charity should be an investment in the poor man's future. You are thus trying to empower him and help him get back on his feet. Here we see a concern that is basic to all imitation of God, namely, concern for human dignity.

Last but not least among the acts of charity/justice is burying the dead. Jacob says to Joseph in Gen 47:29–30: "Do me this favor . . . please do not bury me in Egypt. When I lie down with my fathers, take me up from Egypt and bury me in their burial place."

It is thus a sacred duty to provide for someone's burial. Again the concern is for human dignity.

Honesty

A general statement about honesty is found in Exod 15:26, which reads: "God said, 'If you will heed the Lord your God diligently, doing what is upright in his sight, giving ear to his commandments, and keeping all his laws, then I will not bring upon you any of the diseases that I brought upon the Egyptians, for I the Lord am your healer.'"

Honesty is especially important in commerce and the world of business, as evidenced by the concern with honest measurement of land and honest weights and measures (Lev 19:35). This point is reiterated and made more emphatic by Deut 25:15: "You must have completely honest weights and measures if you are to endure long on the soil that the Lord your God is giving you."

Forgiveness

The history of Israel is replete with acts of forgiveness by God. God may punish Israel, but that too is a sign of God's love. In every case, God insists that Israel admit its fault and beg God's forgiveness. This is the same pattern we see in the book of Judges: Israel sins, God punishes them, Israel repents, God forgives and restores. More or less the same pattern holds for human-human interactions as well. The party who is in the wrong must admit his fault and beg the pardon of the aggrieved party. God readily forgives sins committed against God, but only the aggrieved person can forgive the sin committed against him or her. In any event, those who are insulted or harmed may not retaliate in kind. As Lev 19:18 says, "You shall not take vengeance or bear a grudge against your countrymen. Love your fellow as yourself."

Proverbs 24:17 adds the following: "If your enemy falls, do not exult. If he trips, let your heart not rejoice, lest the Lord see it and be displeased, and avert his wrath from him." This means that the person who exults in his enemy's troubles and refuses to forgive him becomes in God's eyes the guilty party. The idea, then, is to suffer affliction happily, refrain from retaliation, accept the apology when it's offered, and not delay in granting the pardon.

Moderation

As we saw in our discussion of Gen 1:1—2:4a, the things that God has created are good and are therefore meant to be enjoyed. We also saw that God wants us to be happy because only then can God be happy, too. To live in the presence of this loving God is a great joy and delight. There are only two ways to ruin this joy and delight: (1) depriving oneself of life's pleasures, or (2) over-indulging in them. The ideal is to be happy with what one has. Psalm 128:2 puts it succinctly: "You shall enjoy the fruit of your labors; you shall be happy and you shall prosper." That is, if you can be happy with whatever you have, you're rich.

Our Relationship with Animals

Our discussion of Gen 1:1—2:4a showed that we humans are responsible for benevolently and intelligently managing the natural world, a responsibility that applies especially to other animals. God gives them the same blessing God gives us: "Be fruitful and multiply." That shared blessing puts us in a fiduciary relationship with the other animals. That is, we are responsible for their well-being. That responsibility is so serious that one is permitted to violate the Sabbath in order to preserve the life of an animal. Moreover, the Decalogue commands that we also let animals rest on the Sabbath. Deuteronomy 11:15 even says the following: "I [God] will also provide grass in the fields for your cattle—and thus you shall eat your fill." The implication is that a man may not eat his dinner until his cattle are fed.

JEWISH ETHICS AND THE ETHICS OF JESUS OF NAZARETH

My Comments

Such is the ethics of the Hebrew Bible—action that is based upon imitation of God. For this reason, if we observe person 1 behaving more or less according to this ethics, it's not improbable that we might recognize something of God in that person. And if person 2 does an even better job of living according to this ethic, God will be even more recognizable in that person. This idea is perfectly in harmony with what we said in chapter 1, namely, that to the extent we play our role as God's agents on earth, God is able to be present in us and through us.

The way some characters in the New Testament reacted to Jesus of Nazareth indicates precisely this phenomenon. That is, they observed his behavior and concluded that God was present in him. But, as we just learned, the fact that God is recognizable in someone does not make that person God. If people recognized the presence of God in Jesus of Nazareth, what that indicates primarily is that he was doing a very good job of imitating God, just as all humans, especially Jews, are supposed to be doing.

Significantly, however, not everyone who met Jesus of Nazareth saw God present in him. Why was that? It was because Jesus came from the Diaspora-like environment of the Galilee and therefore had liberal ideas that in important ways contradicted the ethics we have just described. He was thoroughly Jewish but in a style that ran against the grain of the reigning orthodoxy. Jesus of Nazareth was the spiritual descendant of those social elements who had always opposed the puritanical and xenophobic Yehud movement and who had produced the biblical literature that challenges the theology that the Yehud movement tried to make normative. Jesus of Nazareth was, in short, an outspoken member of the loyal opposition, and as such, he challenged the dominant ethical norm, usually by seeing how far he could stretch it.

On the question of brotherly love, for example, Jesus demonstrated that one cannot practice brotherly love and separation from Gentiles at the same time; brotherly love is incompatible with any kind of exclusion. Jesus protests against the dominant ethic by fraternizing with and loving all sorts of people who, under the Jewish policy of separation from Gentiles or other sources of impurity, would be excluded. From the perspective of normative Judaism, Jesus' policy of radical inclusion could be seen as a failure to respect group boundaries, as an intentional confusion of the sacred and the profane, and/or as an incitement to assimilation and idolatry.

On the question of charity/justice, Jesus seemed to think that some Jews were perverting charity/justice by using it hypocritically as an excuse for unfaithfulness and self-righteousness or as a vehicle for self-promotion. He taught that the real measure of the worth of charity/justice is not how much a person does or gives but how much the giver has to sacrifice and suffer in order to do it. That's why, for Jesus, the widow's mite is so much more valuable than the large contributions made by the rich. The widow's contribution shows a compassion and self-sacrifice that the rich man's contribution does not.

The Judaism of Jesus' time put a high value on proper motivation, and the Pharasaic movement, from which modern Judaism sprang, put even more value on it. The guiding principle of the Pharisees was that no action could have any religious value unless it was done out of love for God. Thus Jews then and now might very well consider Jesus' attitude toward the doing of charity to be quite admirable. But, at the same time, they might find it so extreme as to be counterproductive because it would have the effect of actively discouraging rich people from doing charity/justice, even though the rich are in the best position to do charity/justice and likewise have the greatest responsibility for doing it. One could very well argue, for example, that the more charity/justice the rich do, the more equitable the distribution of resources that God has loaned to us. Thus Jesus' possibly excessive emphasis on the giver's motivation could be seen as actually impeding justice.

But it's on the question of forgiveness that Jesus most shocks the dominant ethic. He does not believe in the theology of retribution and thus rejects the notion that a person who is poor, sick, or otherwise disadvantaged is being punished by God for his or her sins. Thus Jesus does not ask the poor or the diseased to repent before they can be healed (re-created). Jesus simply heals them or helps them. Their illness is destroyed, and they are re-created. Jesus, acting very much like God as seen in the book of Jonah, unhesitatingly forgives those who ask to be forgiven. For so doing, Jesus is accused of pretending to be God. But if God is actually as forgiving as we see in the book of Jonah and if we are imitators of God, then freely forgiving others is actually just what God expects us human beings to do.

The practical result of Jesus' policy on forgiveness is that he goes beyond the already excellent Jewish idea of refraining from retaliation, of accepting apologies, and of quickly granting pardon. This Jewish idea is very effective at healing damaged relationships at least among Jews, but Jesus is apparently not content with reestablishing the *status quo antes* or with working only among Jews. He wants to use forgiveness as an instrument of destruction/re-creation in cases where the two parties are so seriously estranged from each other that they have no relationship at all or where their relationship is so damaged that the standard Jewish procedure for reconciliation can't manage to heal it. Such would especially be the case in dealing with a crude and cruel non-Jewish enemy, who could not reasonably be expected to give an apology or to engage in the very civilized Jewish rituals of reconciliation. Thus Jesus advises us to skip the usual Jewish formalities, immediately forgive (love) our enemies, and pray for those who persecute us, in the hope that our love and forgiveness will transform those enemies.

In Jewish/Talmudic ethics, making enemies into friends is considered highly desirable, but the Talmud does not provide much help in achieving that end, except what we've already mentioned about protecting the property of one's enemy. In fact, transforming enemies into friends just doesn't receive much emphasis in Talmudic ethics. In any case, the forgiveness Jesus advocates is one in which, inspired by confidence in God, one must risk taking the initiative and bypassing the usual forgiveness protocol, in the hope of transforming dangerous situations and cruel enemies who would never consent to participate in a forgiveness protocol anyway. From the perspective of normative Judaism—and even for many Christians—Jesus' approach might very well be too risky. What's worse, it seems to ignore the whole question of who is at fault and what reparations the guilty party should make. Once again Jesus' radical approach discounts the question of justice. Jesus, like God as seen in the book of Jonah, apparently settles for a universe that is not moral. Jesus is so eager to forgive that the issue of a moral universe just fades away. Given the fact that, by the time of Jesus, the theology of retribution and hence the insistence upon a moral universe had become standard among most Jews, it is not surprising that the Jerusalem authorities considered Jesus to be a dangerous fool.

All things considered, Jesus' ethic is Jewish, but it reflects the values of those Jews who for some five hundred years had opposed the brand of Judaism that the Yehud community made normative. His is an ethic influenced by the ethnically and religiously mixed environment of a Diaspora-like place such as the Galilee, where it was necessary to invent radical ways of turning enemies into friends and where one had to get along with all sorts of people who didn't play by—or even know—the rules of the Jewish community segregated in Jerusalem.

8

Role of Festivals in Postexilic Israel

LET US BEGIN HERE by recalling that, though never explicitly stated, the major challenge facing the Yehud community was to make exclusive loyalty to the God of Israel into a community-wide, popular religion, a goal quite difficult to achieve given the fact that popular religion in preexilic Israel had always been thoroughly polytheistic. The problem was how to encourage individuals to get personally engaged in what was, for most Israelites, a new religion. We argue that festivals played a large role in the solution. If we can understand what the main festivals were/are about, then we will have arrived, via this shortcut, at an understanding of what the Yehud community thought it was attempting to teach and to become. And given the fact that the Yehud community had the most influence in determining the content of the Hebrew Bible, understanding the festivals that the Yehud community instituted means also understanding what the Hebrew Bible is trying to teach.

The first step for the Yehud community was to present the Torah as the foundational document of the community. This is done in Neh 8, where Ezra reads the Torah, or some portion of it, before the public assembly. On the basis of the real history of Israel and the probable date of the Torah's production, it is reasonable to suppose that most people were hearing the Torah for the first time. The people are reported to have responded to the reading by calling out "amen, amen" and by prostrating themselves on the ground. Since the *lingua franca* of the Middle East was by then Aramaic, Levites were present to translate the Hebrew into Aramaic and to explain the text paragraph by paragraph. Nehemiah 8:9 and 12 say that the people responded with a mixture of joy and sorrow. Ezra, however, ordered the public not to rejoice or to mourn but instead to celebrate in a festival meal. The idea was to repeat this public reading and festival meal every year. Then, in Neh 9:38—10:39, the people pledge to observe God's instructions and obey all God's commandments.

Clearly, this pledge could not be kept unless the people were teachable and studied hard. They would have to meet regularly to discuss the Torah. But Torah study might not be sufficient. It is, after all, intellectually demanding, and not everyone is a "text person" or has the leisure time required for study either. Presumably, only a few privileged or very literate people would be able to participate fully in Torah study. Something more than Torah study would therefore be needed to make this religion a regular and active part of people's lives. As suggested above, the answer was festivals, and the peculiar character of these festivals, as we shall see, is that they are all intended to be educational and participatory rather than simply celebratory. Since there was no such educational emphasis in preexilic Israel, apart perhaps from Josiah's call for the celebration of Passover, it is reasonable to infer that the regular celebration of these festivals started only in the postexilic period. More on that in a moment.

It's not possible in this space to present a full-blown description of these festivals. We will have to be content with a discussion of those elements that demonstrate the way these festivals served the Yehud community's need to educate its people in this essentially new religion. For the sake of brevity, we'll limit the discussion to Rosh Hashanah, Yom Kippur, Sukkoth, and Pesach. For the information that follows on the Jewish festivals, we are indebted to Ari Goldman[1] and to Jacob Neusner.[2] My comments are in brackets.

---

1. Goldman, *Being Jewish*, 107–27, 155–63, 188–203.
2. Neusner, *Enchantments of Judaism*, 100–113.

Goldman and Neusner

Rosh Hashanah

[The biblical description of Rosh Hashanah (Num 29:1–2), like the biblical description of the other major festivals, is very brief and doesn't help us very much. For the purposes of discussion we will therefore assume that the Talmud's description of these festivals is more or less in line with the way they were actually celebrated by the postexilic community].

Rosh Hashanah (the New Year) is a one- or two-day festival celebrated in the month of Tishri (usually September). The prayers of the community picture God sitting on the throne of judgment, from which God evaluates and scrutinizes the world. The guiding hope of this festival is for re-creation, which will happen only if God examines people and re-creates them: "Today the world is born," the congregation professes. The worshipper participates by engaging in heartfelt self-examination: Have I lived up to my obligations? Have I loved my neighbor and done charity/justice? Have I been honest, especially in business? Am I reconciled with those against whom I sinned or who sinned against me? Have I done everything I could to achieve this reconciliation? Have I honored my parents? Have I been honest in confessing my sins and symbolically discarding them? Am I seriously committed to living better? After this self-examination, the worshipper asks God to judge him or her. The themes of this festival are divine sovereignty, divine revelation, divine memory, and redemption/re-creation. [We should note that the creation/re-creation theme already indicates that this festival is postexilic in origin. In any case, the themes of this festival represent a fairly comprehensive lesson in the fundamentals of this religion].

Yom Kippur

During the seven days after Rosh Hashanah, Jews are expected to ask forgiveness from anyone against whom they have sinned.

Once they've done that, they are ready for Yom Kippur, the Day of Atonement (Lev 23:27–32). This is the most solemn, personal, and moving day of the year. On this day the individual recites a lengthy and quite detailed alphabetic acrostic (each verse beginning with the next letter in the Hebrew alphabet) prayer of confession. This prayer is constructed as an acrostic so that, in this way, it may humbly offer to God all the letters of the Hebrew alphabet, so that God can form whatever words God chooses. Then the congregation says another prayer of confession, also an acrostic. The purpose of this repetition of confessions is to link the community to the individual and the individual to the community, which takes responsibility for the acts of each of its members. In this way both the individual and the community stand naked, as it were, before God and humbly beg God's love and compassion. On this day, the judgment that God reached at Rosh Hashanah gets written in the Book of Life (finalized). Thus, the theme of this festival is the power of repentance.

[The teaching value of this festival comes largely from the particular ways in which the individual is asked to participate in it]. For example, one fasts in order to learn empathy with the hungry. One abstains from sexual relations in order to learn empathy with the lonely and broken-hearted. One wears cloth shoes—not leather—in order to learn empathy with the poor. One abstains from using any lotions, ointments, creams or perfumes in order to learn empathy with those who can afford no luxuries. One wears white as a symbol of the purity one seeks and as a sign of one's own mortality. Overall this festival teaches solidarity with all humankind and humility before God. [The highly participatory character of this learning experience is striking].

Sukkoth

Five days after Yom Kippur comes Sukkoth, Tabernacles (Lev 23:39–43). While at Rosh Hashanah and Yom Kippur God is pictured as judge, at Sukkoth God becomes a sheltering mother. The sukkah (hut) can be thought of as a kind of divine womb or simply as the hut God provided for the Israelites during the wilderness wandering. Thus Sukkoth is linked to the exodus experience. But it is also a harvest festival that involves four elements from the natural world: citrons (lemons), palm branches, myrtle boughs, and willow branches. [Once again, as we are about to see, the festival is highly engaging]. Each family or community builds a sukkah, which is intentionally flimsy to emphasize their dependence on God and to allow them to see the sky through the roof. The family or families live in the sukkah for a week in order to experience in the flesh the maternal protectiveness of God. One also learns empathy with those who have no home, no shelter. Since everyone from the family or community, rich and poor, young and old, lives in the sukkah, there is, or at least there can be, a marvelous leveling effect. People live together, eat together, sing together, dance together, and share everything. They also learn hospitality by inviting into the sukkah any Jew or really anyone who doesn't have a sukkah. Sukkoth also involves four elements from nature. Their purpose is to teach people to appreciate and protect nature as a gift from God, with emphasis on the responsibility of Jews to preserve nature for future generations. [Once again we see a festival designed for learning by doing].

Pesach

Pesach (Passover: Exod 12:23; Lev 23:6–8) is a seven- or eight-day festival that is highly participatory and directly affects the daily routine of every person because it obligates Jews to eat unleavened bread called *matzah*; not to eat anything leavened or made from wheat, spelt, oats, barley, or rye; and to cleanse their house of everything *chametz*, such as leavened bread or bread-like products. Once that is done, Jews are ready for the Passover *seder*, at which the story of the exodus from Egypt is told through the reading of the *haggadah* (story). Exodus 13:8 commands that this story be taught to children. With hymns, songs, and symbols this story is told [for clearly educational purposes]. This story celebrates that very special moment in time when God destroyed something evil that certainly needed to be destroyed, namely, the very evil social custom or pattern according to which no one could rise above the social station one was born into: anyone born a slave had to remain a slave. God broke that pattern by liberating the Israelites from slavery in Egypt. As a result of being liberated, they were born again. Pesach teaches gratitude to God for all the liberations God has already performed and for all the ones the people hope God will perform in the future. It also teaches empathy with those who need liberation.

The Sabbath

The Sabbath (Exod 20:9) is technically not a festival, but it is considered to be the most impressive and festive of Israel's celebrations. It is celebrated at home from dusk on Friday until dusk on Saturday. It begins when the lady of the house lights candles and sings or recites a psalm (usually Ps 92 or 93). Over the full twenty-four-hour period the participants together share a total of three festive meals, with blessings over the wine and the braided bread (*challah*). At each meal an extra place is set for anyone who might come unexpectedly, for example, a needy person or Elijah announcing the coming of the messiah. At dusk on Saturday, the participants sing a song (the *Havdalah*) which separates the Sabbath from the time that follows. The reason for celebrating the Sabbath at home is to make this rather powerful religious experience as personal as possible and a regular part of people's weekly routine.

The Sabbath incorporates all the themes found in the official festivals: light, joy, revelation, redemption, re-creation, expectation of the messiah, renewal, hospitality, and solidarity with the hungry and the enslaved. The Sabbath teaches that we human beings are worth more than our work and that our destiny is to be at leisure with God. Hence the Sabbath is a time for enjoying what God gives us—including sexual relations—rather than what we humans do for ourselves. Virtually all forms of work are forbidden.

The Sabbath teaches a lesson in ecology as well since on this day Jews relinquish whatever control they have over nature. On this day Jews only observe nature and delight in it but do not attempt to use it. The Sabbath also teaches empathy with all those people or animals that do not have a day of rest.

My Comments

What we have seen is that the major festivals and the Sabbath are all, primarily, experiences in learning by doing. They all teach the basics of this religion, and all have the effect of establishing the identity of the Jewish community. Those who participate in these events and build their lives around them are members of the community. In this way these festivals and the Sabbath forge group cohesion and help establish group boundaries. We can infer that the Yehud community needed a lot of teaching and community building. If the religious ideals of the Yehud community had merely marked the revival of something that already existed and was well-established in people's minds, such pointedly educational activities would not have been necessary. The reality, obviously, is that the Yehud community was attempting to make normative a (for most people) new religion that had to be taught and then strongly reinforced through experiences that not only required active personal participation but made learning that religion a regular part of people's daily, weekly, and annual activities.

If God's plan was to train and educate the Israelites to be the people of God and remain faithful to God over time, it must be admitted that observance of the major festivals and of the Sabbath have worked marvelously well. The Jewish community has had to adapt—and struggle to survive—countless times over the last twenty-five hundred years, but it still celebrates these festivals, still observes the Sabbath, still gathers for Torah study, still performs *mitzvoth*, and still remains faithful to the one true God.

9

Some Practical Implications

IN GEN 1:1—2:4A WE learned that God loves all human beings even more than God loves the rest of the created world. Then, beginning in Gen 12, we saw that God expresses this love especially to Israel, as seen not only in God's promises to Abraham but in the fact that whenever any obstacle threatens to prevent Israel from loving God in return or from becoming a great people through whom all the nations will be blessed, God destroys that obstacle and re-creates Israel individually or collectively. Not all of God's destruction–re-creation cycles are completely effective, but lack of immediate or complete success does not prevent God from continuing to try and eventually succeed in producing the faithful people God always wanted.

Thus, for the people of Israel, there can be absolutely no doubt that they are greatly loved by God and that God will simply not let them fail to respond in kind. Jews understand this and feel loved, and because they do, they do not agonize excessively about what God thinks of them. In the space of seven days from Rosh Hashanah to Yom Kippur, Jews deal honestly and expeditiously with the problem of being in a right relationship with God and with their neighbor, and then they get on with what is the real task at hand, namely, imitating God by doing the good works the Torah commands. They may spend a lot of time studying the Torah, but to know the Torah and then not act upon it is the worst of sins. For

Some Practical Implications

that reason those who study also do: the emphasis is on human agency. Jews see themselves, correctly, as agents of God responsible not only for maintaining the created world but for repairing the damage done to it by human sinfulness. They believe, in accordance with Gen 4:6–7, that we humans, though often sorely tempted to do the wrong thing, have it in our power to do the right thing. Being a Jew is committing oneself not only to knowing but then doing what the Torah says is the right thing.

The situation for Christians is somewhat different, however, because Christianity began at a time when at least some Jews, influenced apparently by Persian religion, came to think of sin not merely as someone's failure to do the right thing but as monstrous evil on a massive scale: sin writ large. In this way sin came to be pictured no longer as simply an evil tendency that each individual had to control but as a cosmic force that no one could manage. In the thinking of the New Testament, this cosmic force actually prevents people from doing the right thing even if they want to do it. Some of the Jews around Jesus apparently had this revised understanding of sin, but they knew that, in the biblical tradition, God does whatever it takes to remove obstacles to people's doing the right thing. Hence sometime after the death of Jesus, the Jews who had been closest to him decided that in suffering and dying, Jesus had been doing battle against this cosmic force called sin and that his being raised from the dead was a clear indication of God's victory over sin. On the cross, God had performed a wonderful destruction in which the power of sin was defeated, and, in the resurrection, Jesus was re-created so as to be no longer merely Jesus but Jesus the Christ. In short, the death and resurrection of Jesus is pictured as the ideal or ultimate destruction/re-creation, and the whole idea in Christianity is that those who cling to Jesus share in his victory over the cosmic force of sin and are re-created.

In this way the followers of Jesus find themselves in a situation strangely like that of Jews. That is, Christians now know that they are greatly loved by God, that God has performed an outrageously spectacular destruction/re-creation for their benefit and for the benefit of all humankind, and that, as long as they identify strongly with Jesus and his victory over sin, there is no longer any force preventing them from imitating God by doing the good works that God commands and that their gratitude to God moves them to do. Occasionally their efforts at doing good works may produce unintended negative consequences, but that fact, while reminding them to exercise due caution, should not in any way prevent them from acting. Therefore, Christians should, like the Jews, not worry about whether God loves them or thinks well of them, because they know very well that God does. Rather Christians should focus on the important task at hand, which is to love God in return by caring for the environment, defending human dignity, correcting injustice, communicating with God, working for peace, and in general repairing the damage that sin has caused to the created world—a concept that both Jews and Christians should have no trouble understanding.

10

Destruction/Re-creation in the New Testament

WE HAVE ALREADY SEEN that the Hebrew Bible pictures the history of Israel as a series of destruction–re-creation cycles that usually involve a favored son simultaneously exalted and humiliated. We have affirmed and briefly demonstrated that this metaphorical understanding of Israel's history dominates the thinking of the New Testament as well. It now seems only fitting to test the validity of that affirmation by examining one of the New Testament gospels, in this case, the Gospel of Mark. We have chosen this gospel because it is the earliest and briefest of the New Testament gospels, and its relative simplicity makes it easier for us to discover its structure. But we would expect to find this same metaphorical structure in Matthew and Luke, too. As preparation for our study of Mark, let us review a number of pertinent ideas that surfaced in previous discussions and that are crucial for reading Mark (All quotations from Mark's Gospel are from the RSV Interlinear Greek-English New Testament).

Jesus of Nazareth can very well be thought of as a spokesman for those Jews who lived far from the centers of power, either in the Diaspora or in Diaspora-like places such as the Galilee, and whose liberal theologies opposed the then-dominant theology of retribution and the xenophobia and sexism of the Jewish authorities in Jerusalem. These liberal Jews had also come to view sin not only as an evil tendency that the individual had to control but also and especially as chaos/death, which God, in creation, had at least tentatively restrained and upon which God would once again have to impose some kind of order. The second pertinent idea is that those Jews who opposed then-normative Judaism considered it and its institutions, particularly the temple, to be thoroughly corrupt. So, then, on to Mark.

Mark begins by identifying Jesus as Son of God, a title which tells us that Jesus is favored by God, and we know from our discussion of the patriarchal narratives that the son who is favored by God can expect to be both exalted and humiliated. Thus this title suggests that God is willing to sacrifice his son Jesus, much as Abraham was willing to sacrifice his son Isaac, with similar provisions for redemption. The imagery of 1:2 adds the notion that Jesus will act as the messenger who leads Israel out of exile. The text implies that, in the mind of these Jews opposed to then-normative Judaism, Israel is in exile, so to speak, alienated from its true self, and that Jesus, because he is favored by God, will be able to rescue Israel through his humiliation/death.

In Mark 1:3, we are reminded that John the Baptist and the Jews around him are definitely a marginalized group, operating very far from centralized authority. They are, in fact, out in the desert on the eastern shore of the Jordan River. John is a Nazirite, that is, a Jew who from birth has been dedicated to serving God. As befits his extremely simple lifestyle, he wears animal skins and eats only wild honey and locusts. John has been baptizing people in the Jordan River. The act of baptizing, involving as it does the important imagery of rescue from the waters, suggests that John is starting a destruction/re-creation that he hopes will eventually include all Israel. In 1:8 we discover that John considers the baptizing he performs with water as only the initial phase of a much more far-reaching destruction/re-creation that will be accomplished only when the baptism that people receive is also spiritual. John is baptizing Jews with water and sending them back across the Jordan into Israel, so that they can be the advance guard that prepares all Israel for spiritual baptism, which is to say, total

Destruction/Re-creation in the New Testament

transformation by God. We can infer that these Jews around John believe that Israel really needs such a transformation. Since, according to the Hebrew Bible, the Israelites originally entered the promised land by crossing the Jordan, John apparently believes that Israel is so corrupt that it must go back to square one and start its history in the promised land anew. Thus, as the baptized cross the Jordan and enter Israel, they are symbolically taking repossession of the promised land and helping Israel start its history in the land all over again.

Now Jesus appears on the scene, and John baptizes him. In this act, Jesus is rescued from the waters—a sign of God's sovereignty over chaos and death. Just as Moses was rescued from the waters, Jesus is rescued so that, like Moses, he can liberate Israel. The implication is that John, Jesus, and the other Jews getting baptized believe that the true Israel is, in some sense, in bondage and needs to be liberated. As Jesus comes up out of the water, God speaks to him, calls him "beloved son," thus confirming our suspicion that Jesus, the one favored by God, will have to undergo the same experience of exaltation and humiliation as so many favored sons in the Bible. God's statement means that Jesus is the one chosen and empowered by God to be God's agent in some large-scale, exodus-like destruction/re-creation, such as John has imagined. The fact that the Spirit of God appears at Jesus' baptism indicates that the spiritual baptism John had hoped for may actually be possible. Importantly, only Jesus hears God's message, and as a result Jesus' identity remains secret. Thus, people who encounter Jesus must discover for themselves who he really is.

If Jesus is going to play his special role, which will inevitably require defeating the cosmic forces of evil, he must first demonstrate that he can control his own sinful tendency and that his loyalty to God is unshakable. For that reason, God leads him into the wilderness for testing at the hands of Satan, who in biblical tradition plays the part of official tester. Jesus passes the test and goes directly to Galilee where, as we've seen in earlier discussions, he can expect to find a receptive audience. The message he preaches is that the kingdom of God is at hand, which is to say that the time has finally arrived when God will transform Israel—and perhaps the whole world—by means of a destruction/re-creation/spiritual baptism. People should therefore repent, Jesus suggests, so that they can be in tune with God's action and prepared for it.

Jesus then invites some men to follow him and be his disciples. Note that these men are not intellectuals or rabbinical students but presumably illiterate fishermen. Their low social status shows that Jesus is very far from the centers of power and religious authority. His is a grassroots movement drawn from among the poor, a fact that also underscores the Diasporan origins of his movement and its alienation from then-normative Judaism, which has its center in Jerusalem and depends heavily on study of the Torah and on education generally.

Having gathered a core group of disciples, Jesus reveals himself to be an observant Jew by going to the synagogue in Capernaum on the Sabbath. He even does some teaching in the synagogue, and people are amazed because he speaks with authority, whereas Jewish teachers are usually much less sure of their answers. While Jesus is still at the synagogue, a mentally ill man appears and asks Jesus if he has come to destroy "them," that is, those possessed by unclean spirits. The man also identifies Jesus as Son of God: the favored son and faithful servant chosen and empowered by God to carry out God's destruction/re-creation. Note that those who are afflicted by cosmic sin recognize Jesus as the one who has come to destroy the power of that sin. In any case, this meeting between Jesus and the mentally ill man is significant because for the first time Jesus comes into direct, personal contact with someone afflicted by sin in the cosmic sense of chaos/death. If Jesus is going to succeed in performing a destruction/re-creation for all Israel, he must first be able to perform it with this mentally ill man. Jesus responds to the man's request by speaking directly to the cosmic force that is making the man ill, and by commanding it to come out of the man. This skirmish with cosmic sin prefigures all of Jesus' subsequent battles against it. People are amazed by this healing. Further causes of surprise for them are that their regular religious teachers do not speak of sin other than in the traditional

Destruction/Re-creation in the New Testament

sense of the individual's evil tendency, and that Jesus speaks with an authority far greater than one can have if one speaks in the standard rabbinical way, which is intentionally open-ended and invites a diversity of opinion.

Jesus heals many people by casting out demons, that is, by authoritatively defeating whatever cosmic sin afflicts them. These events, in which Jesus defeats cosmic sin as it impacts individuals, prefigure the spiritual baptism to which John referred and serve to prepare us for more significant events to come.

In Mark 2:1–12, Jesus heals a paralytic and tells him that his sins are forgiven. Some Jewish religious authorities who witness this event are scandalized because they believe that only God can forgive sin. But Jesus' mission from God requires him to defeat cosmic sin, which is the presumed cause of illness, and when Jesus tells the paralytic that his sins are forgiven, Jesus is simply announcing God's sovereignty over chaos and death. Furthermore, Jesus' God is the generous and freely forgiving God we see in the book of Jonah—not the God who makes forgiveness contingent upon punishment. Here Jesus is consciously imitating his God. For all these reasons, it makes perfect sense for Jesus to claim that he can forgive sin. He is simply imitating his God. Jesus forgives sin by exercising God's own authority over it and thus subduing it. Note that subduing is not the same as eliminating. In Gen 1:1–3, God subdues the forces of chaos and death but does not eliminate them. The fact that God has to continue to perform destruction–re-creation cycles indicates that these evil forces still have the ability to raise their ugly heads and cause trouble. In healing people, Jesus has been putting these evil forces back under a certain control.

In 2:15–17, Jesus dines with tax collectors and sinners, thus breaking the rules of normative Judaism, and, predictably, the Pharisees criticize him for so doing. Jesus responds by explaining that his mission is to heal sick people—that is, those afflicted by sin whether individual or cosmic—and that people who are well don't need him. Thus the text implies once again that Jesus' assignment is to perform a large-scale destruction–re-creation cycle, of which these individual healings are a foreshadowing. The main event is still to come.

In the next episode, John's disciples and some Pharisees who are fasting come to Jesus and ask him why he and his disciples are not also fasting. Jesus responds by saying that he and his disciples are not fasting because his mission is very urgent and his time among them very limited. The motif of urgency is ever-present in all of Mark's Gospel. In fact, the most frequently used word in Mark is "immediately." Thus, the destruction/re-creation that Jesus goes about performing must be urgently needed, and that necessity pushes the action of the story forward at a fast pace.

In previous discussions we saw that Jesus has liberal views on matters such as Sabbath observance. We are not really surprised, then, in 2:23–28, when Jesus and his disciples gather grain on the Sabbath because gathering grain is of course work and for good reason is forbidden on the Sabbath. To some Pharisees who criticize Jesus for thus working, he responds by saying that if people are really hungry and need to gather grain on the Sabbath, it's perfectly permissible since the Sabbath is designed—not to enforce a certain pattern of behavior—but to benefit humans. Jesus is clearly thinking of God not as a lawgiver but as the sensitive and loving God we encountered especially in our discussion of Gen 1:1–2:4a, the God whose happiness depends on the happiness of human beings. Jesus' God suffers whenever humans are suffering. Thus, if someone is suffering from hunger, God wants that person to obtain food even on the Sabbath. Note that such a view of God may not have been normative at the time of Jesus, but it is profoundly and authentically biblical.

To reinforce this point about the Sabbath, Jesus enters the synagogue on the Sabbath and intentionally does what is considered work and is therefore forbidden. That is, he heals a man with a withered hand. While so doing, Jesus explains that nothing could be more lawful on the Sabbath than to save life. Jesus then looks at the Pharisees around him, sees their hardness of heart, and feels sorry for them because they obviously do not understand God the way he does. Thus, the very people who in Jesus' view are

Destruction/Re-creation in the New Testament

most in need of the destruction/re-creation that Jesus is bidden to perform—that is, the Jewish authorities and the Pharisees—do not at all acknowledge their own need for such a transformation. They believe that they are righteous; that they correctly observe the Torah; that Jesus is wrong-headed and dangerous; and that, as a result, he must be killed. Thus, they begin to plot against him. Note, too, that the problem of the Pharisees and of all the Jewish authorities in this gospel is hardness of heart, which is exactly the problem that Pharaoh had in the book of Exodus. It is hardness of heart that makes Pharaoh refuse to let the Israelites leave Egypt. But it is God who intentionally hardens Pharaoh's heart in order to increase the dramatic tension, so that the eventual liberation of the Israelites will give more glory to God. Therefore we suspect that the hardness of heart that Jesus encounters in these religious authorities is also designed to increase the dramatic tension, so that the main event of the destruction/re-creation that God will perform through Jesus will give greater glory to God.

In 3:7–12, Jesus and his disciples withdraw to the sea, and a great multitude from Galilee follows them. Note that crowds, women, the sick, demon-possessed people, and demons themselves understand Jesus very well, but that the religious authorities and those closest to Jesus, particularly his family and his disciples, fail miserably to understand him. His disciples' complete inability to understand him is a terrible irony that frequently provokes Jesus to anger. If the crowds or the sick appreciate Jesus, it's because these poor and bedraggled people suffer much less from any sin of their own than from powerful sin beyond their control. That is, they are the main victims of cosmic sin. Thus, they can recognize and appreciate the one who has come to destroy the power of that sin. The same is true of women and demon-possessed people. Note that women in this story are especially close to Jesus and understand him better than anyone else does; they are in effect his true disciples. Demons also recognize and respect Jesus. They come from the realm of chaos and death, and they remember that God imposed order upon them in creation. They know instinctively that Jesus plans to impose order on them again. Thus, they regard Jesus as their master and fear him.

But why do Jesus' male disciples fail to understand him, in spite of all the private instruction and counseling that Jesus gives them? It's because, although they believe that Jesus has been sent by God to do great things, they don't take seriously Jesus' warning about the great destruction/re-creation that Jesus must carry out; they apparently are not familiar with the biblical motif of the favored son simultaneously exalted and humiliated/killed. When Jesus tells them that, in the coming destruction, he himself must die, the disciples are unwilling or unable to accept the idea that this man sent by God to perform mighty deeds must suffer and die. They are hoping that his demonstrations of power will result in a triumphal ending to this story and that they will richly benefit from being his disciples. But Jesus tells them repeatedly that such is not the case at all and that they themselves should expect to suffer. From the disciples' persistent inability to understand Jesus, we can infer that the hearts of the disciples have also been hardened, a fact that also accounts for their later denial and rejection of Jesus once he is arrested.

In Mark's Gospel we encounter many examples of healing and also a few cases of Jesus' raising people from the dead. We can't comment on all of these, but it may be sufficient to say that they are all forms of destruction/re-creation on the level of the individual. The most significant other example of destruction/re-creation thus far has been Jesus' baptism. But, as a demonstration of destruction/re-creation, even his baptism pales in comparison with what we encounter in 4:35–41, where Jesus and his disciples find themselves in a boat crossing the Sea of Galilee. When a sudden storm arises, the disciples are all scared to death, while Jesus is sound asleep in the stern. They think that he doesn't care if they perish, but he gets up from his nap and rebukes the wind, telling it to be still. The wind immediately grows calm, and all is well. The point of this episode is—not that Jesus can do amazing tricks with the weather—but that, just as God did in Gen 1:1–2, God is again imposing order on the forces of chaos and death, represented by the storm at sea. Thus this episode, with imagery that comes from Gen 1:1–3, is meant to imply that the eventual result of God's action through Jesus will be nothing short of a new creation.

Another episode very similar to calming the storm occurs in 6:45–52. Jesus remains on land, but his disciples attempt to cross the Sea of Galilee by rowboat. They are rowing against a strong wind, and from shore Jesus sees that they are in distress. He then comes walking on the sea to help them. They think they are seeing a ghost, but he identifies himself, calms the wind, and gets into the boat. The point of this episode is that, by walking on the sea, which in ancient Near Eastern mythology is the lair of the chaos monster Mot (Death), Jesus is demonstrating God's dominion over death.

The first ten chapters of Mark's Gospel are devoted to Jesus' mighty deeds, some of which occur in pairs. Thus, we find two episodes of Jesus' calming the wind/sea and two encounters between Jesus and blind beggars (8:22–26 and 10:46–52). Jesus heals them, and the irony is that they "see" who Jesus is, but that his disciples still do not. We also find two stories about Jesus' feeding the multitudes (6:31–44 and 8:1–10). In both cases, the multitudes are poor and hungry, and Jesus feels compassion for them and wants his disciples to feed them. But the disciples believe themselves incapable of such a feat. Jesus has to show them that, because his God is compassionate and committed to the welfare of human beings, especially the poor and down-trodden, nothing is impossible. Thus, Jesus demonstrates the abundant compassion that God has for all humans, especially the poor.

At first, these pairs of similar episodes may seem repetitive or hyperbolic, but, in Mark 8:27–29, immediately after the healing of the blind man in Bethsaida, Jesus makes the first prediction of his suffering and death. This prediction helps us to see that the reason for the text's repetition and accumulation of mighty deeds is to heighten the irony that a man who is the Son of God and who performs such powerful acts must suffer and die.

Importantly, Mark's Jesus is a true man of the people, an earthy and emotional person. He is moved with pity for the sick people he encounters. He feels overwhelming compassion for the multitudes. He is frequently angry with his disciples, and when his main disciple, Peter, fails to accept Jesus' prediction of his own suffering and death, Jesus uses violent language to rebuke him (8:27–33). In fact, scholars have often suggested that Jesus' language in the final form of Mark's text shows every sign of having been cleaned up by some editor. But, even in its present sanitized form, Jesus' language is highly seasoned. In any case, to the extent that Jesus is accurately imitating God, we see how emotional, how candid, and how compassionate God is.

Despite the authority with which Jesus speaks and acts, he somehow does not come across as self-important. For example, Jesus is exhausted after a long and bitter argument with the Pharisees (7:1–23), in which he vehemently rejects the notion of pure and impure foods and says that purity and impurity have to be measured by what comes out of one's mouth—not by what one puts into it. This is a really intense and exhausting confrontation with the Pharisees, and afterward, Jesus wants to get away from people and enjoy some peace and quiet. So he leaves Israel, where the authorities want to engage him in fierce debates, and he crosses over into Tyre and Sidon, which are notoriously polytheistic cities on the Mediterranean coast. He finds a house where he can rest, but before he can even sit down, a woman knocks on the door. As an observant Jew, Jesus is not supposed to have anything to do with a woman who is not his wife, let alone a woman from this heathen place. But he apparently remembers his obligation to imitate God's compassion, and so he opens the door and lets her in. She falls at his feet in a sign of respect and supplication, tells him that her daughter is possessed by an unclean spirit, and begs him to heal her. But Jesus' patience has run out. Annoyed at being disturbed and tired of constant requests, he unthinkingly gives her a short and very nasty reply. He tells her that whatever help he has to offer is reserved for Jews and should not be given to dogs, that is, Gentiles. Undaunted, she humbly accepts the insult, but, determined to find help for her daughter, she tells him that even the dogs may eat the crumbs that fall from the Jews' table. Upon hearing her deeply insightful response, Jesus feels ashamed and

Destruction/Re-creation in the New Testament

embarrassed but also filled with compassion and willing to learn from this Gentile woman.

This episode with the woman from Tyre and Sidon is extraordinary in every way. It shows Jesus tired, cranky, short-tempered, and insulting but also compassionate, open to criticism, and able to take instruction from even the least likely source. Interestingly, even though Jesus has from the very beginning of this gospel spoken with an authority that people find amazing, he does not until now correctly understand his own mission. He thinks that his mission is to liberate the lost sheep of the House of Israel, but this Gentile woman with the mentally ill daughter teaches him that in fact his mission is to liberate all people—not only Jews. The other women in the Gospel of Mark—especially Mary Magdalene, Mary the mother of James, and Salome—all understand Jesus very well and are a great help to him, but this Gentile woman from Tyre and Sidon understands him better than he understands himself and helps him far more than anyone else in this gospel. Thus Jesus is an excellent representative of the biblical tradition that has always opposed the Judaism that became normative under Ezra and Nehemiah, who banished foreign wives and insisted upon separation from Gentiles. The tradition that Jesus represents not only highly values the intelligence, religious insight, and other contributions of women but also believes that at least some Gentiles may know more about God than do Jews.

We know that then-normative Judaism made the temple the center of community life. If Jesus and the Jews who follow him believe that normative Judaism is corrupt, then Jesus must expose the corruption of the temple. So, then, after a long period of activity outside Jerusalem, Jesus finally enters the city in 11:11, goes into the temple, looks around, but decides not to take any action because it's already late in the day, and too few people are there to witness what he might do. On the following day he makes the short walk from Bethany to the temple and on the way sees a fig tree that bears no fruit because it is not the season for figs. This fruitlessness becomes a metaphor for the hard-heartedness of the Pharisees and other religious authorities. Jesus apparently realizes that he is not going to be able to soften their hearts, that his efforts with these people will not succeed, and that the time is not right for their destruction/re-creation. This is an admission and foreshadowing of his own inability to transform those people who are at the core of normative Judaism.

Jesus arrives at the temple, drives out those who are buying and selling, overturns the tables of the money changers and the seats of those who sell pigeons, and does not allow anyone to carry anything through the temple (11:15–16). His actions are clearly illegal and intentionally provocative since these shopkeepers and money changers are only providing the services on which the temple depends for its operation. People from many places visit the temple and have to pay the temple tax to get in, but this tax is payable only in local currency. Hence the need for money changers. Visitors to the temple also buy clean, unblemished animals to sacrifice for their sins. Hence the need for the selling of animals.

But if such commercial activities are all useful and necessary, why does Jesus object to them? The reasons are complicated. On the one hand, the Torah legislates the whole sacrificial system, which is thus holy and good. On the other hand, the eighth-century BCE prophets, especially Amos and Micah, declare that God spurns sacrificial offerings and festivals unless the Jews do justice, love goodness, and walk modestly with God (Mic 6:8). In this verse, Micah summarizes God's expectations for the behavior of all human beings—and especially Jews. Even the most lavish sacrificial offering cannot substitute for the Jews' fulfilling the basic requirement of doing justice, loving kindness, and walking humbly with God. Clearly, Jesus identifies strongly with this prophetic tradition. Thus when he encounters the hard-heartedness and self-righteousness of the Pharisees and religious authorities; or when he sees so many poor and sick people; or when the poor and sick get blamed for their plight; or when he notes that Jews segregate themselves from Gentiles and sinners and withhold God's blessings from them; or when he observes that Jews are using the sacrificial system as an excuse for not honoring their parents (7:9–13), he recognizes that Israel is failing in its responsibilities as the people of God and therefore that their sacrifices in the temple are both futile and offensive to God. Therefore Jesus reminds people that the temple is supposed to be a house of prayer for all the nations—not a den of robbers (11:17).

Another reason for Jesus' opposition to the temple is that his God loves all humans and Jews in particular. Temple sacrifices seem very much like attempts to win God's favor, but Jesus knows that God's favor does not need to be won. Therefore, in Jesus' opinion, the whole sacrificial system is a misunderstanding of the very nature of the God whom Jesus knows. What's worse, the sacrificial system certainly looks like a throwback to the polytheistic religions, in which one had to propitiate the gods through sacrifices of various kinds. Thus the sacrificial system is anachronistic and corrupt by its very nature, above and beyond the fact that God spurns sacrifices that are not matched by sincere imitation of God. To the extent that the temple exists for the sake of sacrifices, it also is corrupt, and, for all of the above reasons, so is then-normative Judaism.

Let us return now to the question of the major destruction/re-creation that Jesus has been sent to perform: freeing Israel—and all humanity—from bondage. In cases of illness or blindness, Jesus heals by exercising God's sovereignty over the forces of chaos and death. More spectacularly, Jesus raises Jairus' daughter from the dead (5:35-43) and twice shows God's dominion over wind and water. These actions foreshadow, but certainly do not constitute, the main event. Three times Jesus predicts that this event will require him personally to suffer and die (8:31; 9:31; 10:33). As we struggle to grasp the significance of these predictions, we realize that when a sick man goes through a destruction/re-creation, his sick self dies, and his healthy self is born. But that transformation takes place only within and for the benefit of that individual. How is it that Jesus' predicted suffering and death are supposed to benefit others? How can the destruction/re-creation of an individual have a generalized, even cosmic effect?

The answer to this question lies in another biblical concept of which the author of this gospel is quite fond. It's the Suffering Servant,[1] a thought that comes from the school of the prophet Isa-

---

1. I am well aware that most New Testament scholars believe that Suffering

iah. The background for this notion is the exile in Babylon, during which Israel is so far from Jerusalem and so traumatized that it loses its identity. Thus the nations think that Israel has been annihilated. But God commissions a servant to lead Israel back to Jerusalem on a highway that God opens through the desert. In this way, God uses the servant to restore Israel's identity. The Suffering Servant is all Israel or possibly an individual who personifies all Israel. But we can also recognize that the idea of a Suffering Servant is a variation on the motif of the favored son, whose existence is marked not only by exaltation but also and especially by suffering and humiliation.

As the term Suffering Servant implies, this servant has a tough job. He must silently, uncomplainingly bear the consequences of the sins of others by allowing himself to be insulted, rejected, and tortured. The servant does not literally die, but he bears the death-like guilt of all Israel. As a result of the Suffering Servant's action, Israel is able once again to enjoy the land that God promised them. Because of the Suffering Servant, Israel will become the land of righteousness and justice, steadfast love and fidelity. This is good news, and the prophet will announce it—not to the rich and powerful—but to the poor and humble, because the rich unjustly kept the poor from their reward (Isa 60:17—61:8). We suspect that it is also because the rich are strangely deaf to this message. Like Pharaoh, their hearts are hardened, so that when the poor finally receive their just reward, God will be all the more glorified.

If Jesus is being portrayed in this gospel as the prophet who announces good news to the poor, we can appreciate why he has humble origins, why his disciples are simple fishermen, why he values the widow's mite, why he heals the sick, why he preaches to the poor and feeds them, why he is understood and respected primarily by people of low social status, including women. And if he is also portrayed as the favored son/Suffering Servant, we can understand why he is arrested, insulted, rejected, and tortured.

Servant imagery is not to be found in Mark or Matthew and that it appears first in Luke. But the Suffering Servant motif is actually just a variation on the already well-established theme of the favored son who is simultaneously exalted and humiliated. That is, the notion of the Suffering Servant simply represents the application of the favored son theme to Israel personified.

Destruction/Re-creation in the New Testament

As both the favored son/Suffering Servant and the prophet/messenger who announces good news to the poor, Jesus goes through the Gospel of Mark both announcing good news and taking upon himself the consequences of everyone's sin, whether individual or cosmic. As the favored son/Suffering Servant, Jesus personifies the true Israel. Note that, in this role, Jesus is humble and anti-heroic because God requires it (Mic 6:8) and because servants of God in the Bible usually are humble and anti-heroic. Moses, Gideon, and Jeremiah, for example, are all painfully aware of their inadequacy. David, too, comes from humble origins.

Since the favored son or the Suffering Servant in Isaiah has to suffer greatly but doesn't die, we can understand why Jesus' disciples have trouble accepting Jesus' predictions of his own death. The secret of Jesus' identity is that, contrary to expectations surrounding the favored son/Suffering Servant, Jesus must die. But why exactly must he die? If sin were strictly individual, Jesus could go around forgiving everyone's sin, and his job would be done. But we see in his conversations with demons and in his demonstrations involving the wind and the sea that his principal challenge comes from cosmic sin, which is a problem that previous favored sons or Isaiah's Suffering Servant didn't have to struggle with. It is such a monstrous problem, in fact, that even a near-death experience for Jesus would seem insufficient and that his actual death would be required.

As the time for Jesus' main event approaches, he invites his male disciples to celebrate the Passover meal with him. During dinner, he predicts that one of them will betray him, but this prediction is much too optimistic because in fact all his male disciples will soon betray and abandon him. More importantly, this scene emphasizes the words that Jesus speaks over the bread and wine. He tells them that this bread is his body. Here, we remember that Jesus is playing the role of the true Israel, that is, the Israel that God always intended—not the Israel of then-normative Judaism. Thus, by eating Jesus' body, his disciples will become the true Israel. This invitation to eat Jesus' body may also remind us of the fact that Jesus felt enormous compassion for the hungry multitudes and fed them—not simply out of compassion for their hunger but out of a desire to see them, too, participate in the true Israel. As Jesus prepares for his forthcoming confrontation with the forces of chaos and death, he feeds his own disciples by giving them this bread as his own body, so that eating this bread will inextricably link his disciples to him. In this way, his disciples will become favored sons, too, with all that term suggests of exaltation and humiliation. He then tells his disciples to drink the wine, which he calls his blood. Here, we think of the exodus event, in which the Israelites spread the blood of a lamb on their doorposts so that the destruction will spare them. The implication is that those who eat this bread and drink this wine will be marked with the blood of the sacrificial lamb and thus be both spared and liberated, just as the Israelites were liberated from Egyptian bondage. The Suffering Servant imagery adds the idea that Jesus' followers will be led out of exile and regain their identity as the true Israel. Both sets of imagery imply that Jesus' followers will constitute a new creation. That is the good news. The harsh reality that accompanies this good news is that Jesus has repeatedly told his disciples that if they wish to follow him, they must imitate him. Thus eating the bread and drinking the wine also imply a willingness to suffer and die as God's favored sons.

Immediately after this meal, Jesus goes to the garden of Gethsemane with his disciples and invites them to stay awake with him to pray. By falling asleep, they symbolically abandon him, and, once he is arrested, they literally abandon him. Peter, his favorite disciple, even publicly denies knowing him.

Let us pause to recall that our aim in this discussion of Mark's Gospel is to understand how Mark uses the metaphor of destruction/re-creation, which usually involves the motif of the favored son and which forms the literary structure of Israel's experience with God in the Hebrew Bible. We have discovered that this gospel tells a story quite similar to the Exodus narrative, so similar in fact that Mark's Gospel seems patterned after it.

In chapter 3 of the book of Exodus, Moses is tending his father-in-law's sheep in the desert, which in the Hebrew Bible is the ideal locale for an encounter with God. Moses encounters God, who chooses him to be God's agent in the liberation of Israel. When Moses goes to Pharaoh and tries to convince him to let the Israelites go, God hardens Pharaoh's heart. Because Pharaoh's heart is hardened, the process that leads to Israel's eventual liberation is full of obstacles and thus very painful and slow, allowing abundant opportunity for the God of Israel to demonstrate his superiority over the gods of the Egyptians. Finally, and for a brief moment, Pharaoh relents and allows the Israelites to depart—but then changes his mind, so that God, by opening a pathway through the sea, has the opportunity to dramatically exercise his sovereignty over the chaos monster Mot, too. As a result, God is spectacularly glorified. But Moses does not have to die; it is sufficient for him to have only a near-death experience.

Similarly, in the opening chapter of the Gospel of Mark, Jesus finds himself in the desert with John, and there God declares him to be the favored son and chooses him to be God's agent in the liberation of Israel. In the first ten chapters, Jesus has some notable successes in carrying out his mission, but the authorities he confronts have hearts that God has hardened. As a result, the authorities block Jesus every step of the way and plot to murder him judicially. In this way, the religious authorities play the role of Pharaoh, so to speak; they make certain that none of Jesus' successes, however spectacular they may be, are sufficient for his accomplishing the task that God has assigned to him. That is, the hard-heartedness of the authorities forces Jesus into a more dangerous and demanding situation than even Moses had to face. It is not enough for Jesus to be a new Moses and have a near-death experience; he must actually die. If the authorities were to relent, his death might not be necessary, but they do not relent. Thus Jesus recognizes early on in this gospel both that he will have to die and also that he is failing to transform those people who are at the core of then-normative Judaism. The disciples find it sad and unacceptable that Jesus should have to die, but, from the standpoint of creating a situation in which God is going to be glorified even more than in the exodus, Jesus' death is necessary and even good.

One of the interesting peculiarities of Mark's Gospel is that Jesus' disciples fail utterly to understand him and eventually abandon and deny him. Thus we infer that God has hardened their hearts, too. But for what reason? The answer seems to be that God wants to be glorified not only for exercising his sovereignty over the forces of chaos and death and thus liberating human beings from the power of sin, but also for freely forgiving sinners. It is important for God not to be thought of as insisting that sinners be punished in order to be forgiven. Therefore, in this gospel, Jesus must necessarily find himself in a situation in which he can demonstrate such radical forgiveness. Ideally, in order to give Jesus such an opportunity, people beloved by Jesus would sin grossly against him, so that he could then freely forgive them and thus underscore God's forgiving nature, in contrast with the profoundly false image of God that emerges from the theology of retribution. Jesus' male disciples, especially Peter, are very dear to Jesus, and having failed to understand him and having abandoned and denied him, they are exactly the gross sinners that the situation requires. But how does Jesus show that he forgives them?

After Jesus' death on the cross, his body is buried and lies in the grave three days. That length of time tells us that Jesus is completely in the power of the monster Death, whose tentacles hold him captive, and that it is not certain that Jesus will be released. In this way, fears mount, doubts increase, uncertainty pervades, just as in the Exodus narrative. Thus, just as in the Exodus narrative, everything is set for God to be glorified. Importantly, Jesus' male disciples are all in hiding, and it is two female disciples, Mary Magdalene and Mary the mother of James, who discover where he is buried. Early Sunday morning just after sunrise, these two women and Salome bravely visit the tomb and bring spices to anoint the body. They are surprised to find the heavy stone door of the tomb already rolled away. When they go in, they find a young man dressed in white robes. He tells them that Jesus is risen from the dead and is not there and that they should tell the disciples—and Peter—to meet him in Galilee. This message for the disciples indicates that Jesus has already forgiven them, even the intransigent

Peter, and is giving them a second chance to be his disciples. This message is also important because, by telling his disciples to meet him in Galilee—rather than Jerusalem—Jesus is frankly admitting his failure to transform then-normative Judaism. The meeting in Galilee suggests that Jesus' message has no future in Jerusalem. It will be meaningful only for people in Galilee and beyond. At this point, the three women flee from the tomb and are so frightened that they say nothing to anyone, and the original text of Mark's Gospel ends (16:8).

We can conclude, then, that this gospel has the same imagery, structure, and theme as the Exodus narrative and that, like the Exodus narrative, it is a story focused on God. Christians tend to think that it is mainly about Jesus, but it is no more about Jesus than the Exodus narrative is about Moses. Jesus and Moses are God's favored sons, servants, and messengers, and their role is not to seek their own glorification but to act in such a way that God is glorified. Jesus says as much in 14:36, which reads: "Abba, Father, all things are possible for you. Remove this cup from me. Yet not what I want but what you want."

The Gospel of Mark is the story of God's attempt to perform a destruction/re-creation upon normative Judaism in the time of Jesus, and Mark uses the imagery of destruction/re-creation from beginning to end. Every single episode involves destruction/re-creation. Mark uses the imagery surrounding the favored son/Suffering Servant and the messenger in order to highlight the themes of Israel's returning from exile and recapturing its true identity. Mark patterns itself after the Exodus narrative in order to emphasize the theme of liberation from bondage. Mark uses God's hardening of hearts, another destruction/re-creation motif from the Exodus narrative, to build dramatic expectation, to put the focus squarely on the final resolution of the plot, and to glorify God. Mark uses the favored son motif to show that God is sacrificing his only son for the sake of the true Israel, and Mark uses the resurrection to show that God both sacrifices his son and, at the same time, spares him. In this way, Mark makes the fullest possible use of favored son imagery: Jesus is exalted in his first appearance in the gospel. Later he willingly agrees to be humiliated and murdered, and precisely because of his willingness to put God above everything and everyone else, Jesus is once again exalted.

Note that, from chapter 3 of Mark onward, this attempt by God to transform then-normative Judaism is doomed to failure because of the hard-heartedness of the authorities. But as the one who hardens hearts for his own purposes, God is aware of the inevitable failure of this mission, and so is Jesus. But God goes ahead anyway, and Jesus obediently and willingly follows through with it to the bitter end. The result is that, although then-normative Judaism is not transformed, God destroys the power of cosmic sin and keeps it under his control and supervision. This is good news for everyone and especially for those who are in communion with Jesus. Those who hear this news and take it to heart are transformed (4:26–32). The second piece of good news is that, especially through Jesus' pardon of his disciples, Jesus reveals God to be completely free to love and to forgive, without in any sense being restricted by the theology of retribution. The third piece of good news is that Jesus announces this good news to his intransigent disciples, to the poor, to the sick, to women, and to anyone else who wants to hear it, especially Gentiles. These are the ones whom God in this gospel liberates from bondage and leads out of exile. They are God's new creation.

Because we have been trying to demonstrate that the motif of the favored son simultaneously exalted and humiliated/killed and the metaphor of destruction/re-creation are central to the structure of Mark's Gospel, let us reiterate that Jesus is the ideal favored son—the Son of God—and that his death and resurrection are a parade example both of humiliation followed by exaltation and destruction followed by re-creation. On the cross, the man Jesus dies / is destroyed, along with the weight of sin that he is carrying, and in the resurrection he is reborn as the Christ. Thus, he constitutes the firstfruits of God's new creation.

Fairly or unfairly, this gospel leaves us with the conclusion that the Judaism of Jesus' time is God's incorrigible and moribund old creation. But we should bear in mind that if God is the one who hardens hearts for his own purposes, then the destruction/re-creation that God performs through and on Jesus should be seen primarily as God's attempt to announce good news to Gentiles rather than as a condemnation of Jews. Historically, God has never hesitated to perform a destruction–re-creation cycle on Jews whenever God felt it was necessary and appropriate. Whether God did not really intend to transform first-century CE Judaism through Jesus of Nazareth or whether God simply failed in the attempt is unknowable. In any case, for Christians, the appropriate emphasis is on what God has done for Gentiles.

Glossary

Abraham, his son Isaac, and Isaac's son Jacob—These are the so-called "patriarchs" or ancestors of Israel. The Hebrew Bible implies that they lived in the early second millennium BCE.

Abram (Abraham) and Sarai (Sarah)—In response to a call from God, this childless couple leaves home and family in Mesopotamia and sets out on a journey with God toward an unknown destination. They are the legendary progenitors of the Israelites.

Adam, Eve, Cain, and Abel—These are the first named humans to appear in the Hebrew Bible. They are ahistorical but representative figures.

Ahaz—As the father of Hezekiah and a king of Judah (742–727 BCE), he was known for submitting to Assyrian influence and thus encouraging polytheism.

Ammon and Moab—These were both neighboring states that were unfriendly to Israel.

Amon—He was the son of Manasseh and a king of Judah (643–641 BCE) who was assassinated.

Ananias—He was a relative of Nehemiah who, late in the fifth century BCE, was the Yehud envoy to the Diaspora.

Arameans—These were members of a tribe of wandering Semites who appeared on the scene in Israel around 1100 BCE.

Glossary

Artaxerxes—He was king of Persia in the mid-fifth century BCE, and he sent Ezra to Jerusalem with the mission of purifying religious practices there.

Babylonian Exile—When the Babylonians invaded Judah in the early sixth century BCE, they destroyed the temple and took Jerusalem's elite citizenry into exile in Babylon. The exile lasted from 598 to 539 BCE.

Cyrus—As a late-sixth-century BCE king of Persia and the founder of the Persian Empire, his decree authorized the Israelites exiled in Babylon to return to Jerusalem and rebuild the temple.

David and Solomon—They were historical kings of the legendary united kingdom that included both the northern and southern kingdoms. According to traditional chronologies, they lived in the tenth century BCE.

Deuteronomistic History—This was the first continuous history of Israel. Ranging from the book of Deuteronomy through 2 Kings, it was written during the reign of Josiah (639–609 BCE) and was then reedited by the Yehud community sometime after 539 BCE.

Elephantina—This was a Persian military outpost on the southern border of Egypt during the period of Persian military occupation (ca. 539–332 BCE).

Esau—He is Jacob's brother. Jacob swindles Esau out of his brother's rights as firstborn son such that Jacob continues in Abraham's line instead of Esau, who drops out of sight and becomes the legendary father of the Edomites.

Gideon—He is an Israelite general with a large army. God convinces him to go to war against the Midianites despite having only a few men armed with torches and kitchen jars; nevertheless, Gideon wins a great victory that glorifies God.

Hezekiah—He was a king of Judah (727–698 BCE) known for attempting religious reform.

Glossary

Jeremiah—He was a great sixth-century prophet who initially resisted his call, claiming that he was too young and too inarticulate to be a prophet.

Jeshua—As another Israelite leader returned from exile, he was an associate of Zerubbabel. Together, they rebuilt the altar in the temple sometime after 520 BCE.

Jesus of Nazareth—Jesus is an itinerant preacher and healer whom John recognizes as the one sent by God to perform a baptism—not by water, but by the Spirit of God.

Job—He is a rich and righteous Gentile. In response to Satan's insinuation that Job is loyal to God only because God has blessed him so abundantly, God agrees to subject Job to a loyalty test administered by Satan. Because of this test, Job suffers greatly but does not curse God, even while Job's "friends" believe he is being punished for sins that he refuses to admit. God eventually intervenes, rebukes Job's critics, and, in the most extravagantly generous way, compensates Job for his loyalty during the ordeal.

John—Also known as John the Baptist, he is an Israelite who has been dedicated entirely to God since birth and who now lives in the desert where he wears animal skins, eats wild honey and locusts, and baptizes people in the Jordan River.

Jonah—He is an Israelite who believes strongly that sinners should be punished. God calls him to travel to Nineveh to preach repentance to the Ninevites, who are notoriously evil and sinful, but Jonah refuses to accept this assignment and flees from God because he strongly suspects that God will in fact pardon the Ninevites. Finally, Jonah preaches to the Ninevites, who immediately repent. God then forgives them, and Jonah has a hard time accepting God's decision.

Joseph—He is a late born son of Jacob. Joseph's brothers sell him into slavery in Egypt, where he becomes second-in-command to Pharaoh and, in this position, saves Jacob's family (Israel) from a famine in Canaan. Jacob then re-settles the

Glossary

Israelites in the richest agricultural area in Egypt, where the Israelites experience significant population growth.

Josiah—He was the son of Amon and a king of Judah (639–609 BCE) who was famous for conducting religious reform and promoting literary production.

Leah and Rachel—These are Jacob's wives. Although Jacob loves Rachel, he is tricked into marrying Leah too.

Manasseh—He was the son of Hezekiah and a king of Judah (698–643 BCE) who was infamous for promoting polytheism.

Mary Magdalene, Mary the mother of James, and Salomé—These women support Jesus, understand him, take care of him, and remain much more loyal to him than his male disciples.

Mesha—He was a ninth-century BCE king of Moab.

Moses—He is the child of Israelites but is rescued from the Nile by Pharaoh's daughter and raised in her father's court. He eventually becomes aware of his solidarity with Israelites, kills an Egyptian who is attacking an Israelite slave, and then flees to the Sinai desert, where he marries the daughter of a Midianite named Jethro and, while tending Jethro's sheep, meets God near a burning bush. God sends him to tell Pharaoh to let the Israelites leave Egypt.

Nebuchadnezzar—He was the Babylonian king who invaded Judah around 600 BCE.

Necho—He was an Egyptian Pharaoh and a contemporary of Josiah.

Nehemiah—He was sent by Artaxerxes in 445 BCE to rebuild the city walls of Jerusalem.

Ninevites—These were citizens of the notoriously sinful Babylonian city of Nineveh.

Noah—In a mythological period of horrific human sinfulness, Noah is a good and righteous man. God destroys all living creatures except Noah's family and the creatures on his ark. God then re-creates the human species by using Noah and his three sons: Shem, Ham, and Japheth. Israel descends from Shem (Semites).

Glossary

Peter—Peter is a fisherman who becomes a disciple of Jesus but misunderstands him and later betrays/denies him.

Rahab—She is a Canaanite prostitute who welcomes and protects a team of Israelite spies sent to reconnoiter Canaan on the eve of the Israelites' legendary invasion and conquest. She displays enormous courage and cleverness and a great knowledge of God's plans and intentions.

Rehoboam—As Solomon's son and successor, he is known for provoking the dissolution of Solomon's legendary united kingdom.

Ruth—The heroine of the book of Ruth, she is a Moabite whose Israelite husband died in Moab. She bravely follows her widowed mother-in-law to Israel, where Ruth displays amazing loyalty to and knowledge of the God of Israel, by whose hidden hand she marries Boaz and becomes the great-grandmother of King David.

Sheshbazzar—He was the leader of the first group of Israelites to return to Jerusalem from the Babylonian exile. He directed the rebuilding of the temple (completed in 515 BCE).

Yehud—This was the official name of Israel during the period when it was a province of the Persian Empire (539–332 BCE).

Zedekiah—He was the last king of Judah and was taken into exile in Babylon, where he was blinded.

Zerubbabel—He was an associate of both Sheshbazzar and Jeshua, and he has been credited with reestablishing worship after the exile.

Bibliography

Cohen, Abraham. *Everyman's Talmud*. New York: Schocken, 1949.
Finkelstein, Israel, and Neil Asher Silberman. *The Bible Unearthed*. New York: Touchstone, 2002.
Goldman, Ari. *Being Jewish*. New York: Simon & Schuster, 2000.
Hyers, Conrad. *The Meaning of Creation: Genesis and Modern Science*. Atlanta: John Knox, 1984.
Jewish Publication Society. *JPS Hebrew-English Tanakh: The Traditional Hebrew Text and the New JPS Translation*. Philadelphia: Jewish Publication Society, 1999.
Levenson, Jon D. *The Death and Resurrection of the Beloved Son*. New Haven: Yale University Press, 1993.
Nestle, Eberhard. *The RSV Interlinear Greek-English New Testament: The Nestle Greek Text with a Literal English Translation*. Translated by Alfred Marshall with a foreword by J. B. Phillips. London: Bagster, 1958.
Neusner, Jacob. *The Enchantments of Judaism*. New York: Basic, 1987.
Schama, Simon. *A História dos Judeus: Encontrar as Palavras, 1000 A.C.–1492 D.C.* Lisbon: Círculo de Leitores e Temas e Debates, 2013.
Westermann, Claus. *Creation*. Philadelphia: Fortress, 1974.

www.ingramcontent.com/pod-product-compliance
Lightning Source LLC
Chambersburg PA
CBHW070929160426
43193CB00011B/1632